THE DINO STORY

BY Jeanette Lockerbie
Tomorrow's at My Door
The Image of Joy
"Just Take It From the Lord, Brother"

WITH Dino Kartsonakis
The Dino Story

THE DINO STORY

DINO KARTSONAKIS

with Jeanette Lockerbie

Fleming H. Revell Company
Old Tappan, New Jersey

Scripture quotations not otherwise identified are from the King James Version of the Bible.

Scripture quotations identified LB are from The Living Bible, Copyright © 1971 by Tyndale House Publishers, Wheaton, Illinois 60187. All rights reserved.

The verse beginning: "God has His best things for the few" is taken from "Days of Heaven on Earth," by A. B. Simpson, and used by permission of Christian Publications, Inc., Harrisburg, Pennsylvania 17101.

Lines from "There's Something About That Name" © Copyright 1970, by William J. Gaither. Used by permission of Gaither Music Co.

Lines from "The Savior Is Waiting" by Ralph Carmichael.©Copyright 1958 by Sacred Songs (A Div. of Word, Inc.). Used by permission.

Library of Congress Cataloging in Publication Data

Kartsonakis, Dino.
   The Dino story.

   1. Kartsonakis, Dino. I. Lockerbie, Jeanette W. II. Title.
ML417.K3A3   786.2'1'0924 [B]   75-4518
ISBN 0-8007-0733-8

Copyright © 1975 by Fleming H. Revell Company
All rights reserved
Printed in the United States of America

TO
*my grandmother
and all those who have backed
my ministry in prayer*

Contents

	Foreword	9
	Acknowledgments	11
1	When It All Began	13
2	Meet the World's Finest Mother	19
3	The First Girl in My Life	27
4	Thank God for Miss Smith	38
5	Our Boy, Dino	45
6	Miracles—You Better Believe It!	51
7	I Knew Dino When . . .	64
8	Everybody Should Have Such a Grandmother	73
9	What Am I Doing in the Army, Lord?	81
10	Keeping the Balance	89
11	It Took a Miracle	96
12	Taking and Making Opportunities	102
13	What More Can a Secretary Ask?	109
14	On the Go With God	115
15	It <u>Can</u> Happen to You	123

Foreword

The first time I met him was in 1969 in the plush foyer of a high-rise office building that soars above what is affectionately called the Sunset Strip, just before it swoops down among the mansions and manors of Beverly Hills. It's a glass-and-chrome area peopled by talent executives, personal managers, advertising agents, and other show-business stalwarts who attempt to guide the careers of talented unknown performers from a cramped apartment somewhere in West Hollywood to those same Beverly Hills estates—a short journey geographically, but for all too many, one that cannot be navigated even in a lifetime.

Dino had just come from New York City to play a concert for a young-people's convention. The reaction to his piano artistry had been outstanding; and now, here he was—an incredibly gifted and handsome young man with all of the charm and appeal that I so often think is a Greek monopoly—sharing with me his desire to use his talent exclusively for the glory of God.

For a split second I hesitated, the muted sound of traffic along the boulevard of stardom a reminder of the temptations to "cash in" on his talent that would surely come his way, threatening his resolve that it be set apart for sacred use.

"Can he take it?" I wondered. I knew that he had all the potential for a great future for God. But would he have the maturity, the special stability that only a talented performer can fully appreciate during those crucial moments of truth when *career* often carries the price tag of *compromise?*

Then I saw the glint of Christian conviction in his flashing eyes, a devotion rare among young men. And I knew he could take it.

To say that the intervening years have verified my conclusion would be an oversimplification. I have watched the magnificent growth and maturing of this young man, seen him perform under every conceivable type of circumstance, and been constantly amazed at a stability far beyond his years. His keyboard virtuosity remains a dedicated and consecrated talent which is constantly being offered as a love gift to the One who so graciously gave him the talent at the beginning.

Dino is living proof that: ". . . he which hath begun a good work in you will perform it until the day of Jesus Christ" (Philippians 1:6).

On that, I'll stake my life.

KATHRYN KUHLMAN
PITTSBURGH, PENNSYLVANIA

Acknowledgments

First, I want to acknowledge publicly that I am what I am by the grace of God. All the talent I have, *God* gave me. And I want to thank Him for His marvelous direction and guidance in my life.

To *Miss Kathryn Kuhlman* who has so graciously written a foreword for the book, I am indebted and grateful.

To my own family, my pastor, and my friends whom you will meet in these pages, a big "thank you" for being so willing to share in order to give broader dimensions to the book.

Then to my coauthor, *Jeanette Lockerbie*, without whose skill and talent this book would not have been written. Thank you, Jeanette. It's been fun as well as an inspiration to work with you. Sometimes I could feel you crawling into my mind!

And to our publisher, Fleming H. Revell Company, a word of thanks to each one who has worked in the preparation and production of *The Dino Story*.

DINO KARTSONAKIS

1
When It All Began

"Except you become as a little child..." (*see* Matthew 18:13).

The title of this book, *The Dino Story*, could be misleading. It would be indeed, if the focus were on me, Dino, and not on the Lord Jesus Christ.

But, rather, it's my wish and prayer that as people read it, they will come to see, to *experience*, what a relationship with Jesus really is; what He has meant in my life. I mean the personal walk with Him, this consistent, unchanging relationship. Not a matter of periodically getting down on my knees for an hour—or ten minutes; or of being faithful in attending church. No! It's more, so much more than that. It's sensing the presence of Christ with me every second, every minute of the day. When this happens in our lives, the subconscious mind absorbs it to the degree that, even though the conscious might be off guard, the subconscious takes over, keeping one's spiritual life intact. It's this steady, stable "always" relationship with Christ. That's what I mean by *consistent*.

In my own life this spiritual awareness began to develop when I was a very young child. It was at the age of seven, in Glad Tidings Tabernacle in New York City, I remember accepting Christ as my personal Saviour. It's as clear to me today as it was that Sunday afternoon. My mother and my sister and I practically lived in church all day Sunday (as well as attending all the weeknight services). We had our regular pattern. At that time my father was not yet living for the Lord, and my mom, my sister, and I would leave our home on Sixty-third Street and Amsterdam Avenue in time to have our weekly treat. I can remember it yet—Sunday breakfast at the Automat on Thirty-third Street right near our church (also near Pennsylvania Station). This was a gathering place for our church people. I've heard it said that this particular Automat thrived on the Glad Tidings' customers. Mom tells to this day the experiences she and my sister had with me there. I would insist on carrying the tray with the food. We preferred to eat on the balcony and regularly, according to Mom and Chris, I would tumble down the flight of stairs, tray, dishes, food, and all. "Guess who?" they would say to each other as they heard the clatter. My sister says she grew up wondering if everybody's brother was as clumsy as hers! But their embarrassment must not have gotten to me, for I have vivid, happy memories of those breakfasts; so much so that, when I'm back in New York City, if it's at all possible, I go to that Automat and relive the good times.

Our first service was at 10 A.M. My mother was a church soloist; my sister sang also, and I was accompanying them before my feet could reach the pedals of the piano.

Two to three o'clock was the Sunday-school hour, followed by the major service of the week: the great preaching service from three to five P.M. The afternoon emphasis was because our church attracted many from the suburbs and this was the most convenient time for most of them.

But five o'clock was still early in the day for our Glad Tidings' folk. We had a break for dinner, then out on the street we went for a meeting. We loved those street meetings. Some people have asked me at times, "Didn't you ever feel embarrassed out there on a New York City street, singing and playing your accordion and witnessing?"

Embarrassed? That was *our way of life*, to serve the Lord, even as children. We didn't know anything about what other people thought or felt about us. I suppose if we thought about it at all, we probably figured every child would be delighted to be as fortunate as we were. We were in the heart of everything in our church and we revelled in it all.

Next, we had the Christ's Ambassadors—our young-people's groups. Then into the great evening preaching service from 7:30 until—the preacher finished! Sometimes it was 9:15, sometimes much later.

Because I was just a little kid, I know I slept through some of the services. But *I was there*, at every one. And this has had a tremendous influence on my life. I was immeasurably fortunate to have a mother who stood right by my sister and me, always concerned over our spiritual life and our growth and development in Christ.

We frequently had visiting evangelists at Glad Tidings. Though I don't remember the one who was preaching on that particular Sunday afternoon when I was seven years old, I must have been listening very intently. He was speaking on total commitment—giving your life over to Jesus—giving your talents to Him for Him to use. And when he gave the invitation I was the first one to stand up and then run down to the altar. I can still remember standing there looking up into the eyes of the evangelist and him looking down at me. And I recall that he nodded down to me, indicating, "Yes, I know you want to give your life to Jesus, give your talents to Him." (No doubt this man had heard something about this child prodigy. The church people tended to think I was a pretty good little pianist then. So I assume they had talked about the little kid who was using his ability that God had given him, serving in the church.)

That was the day! And it is indelibly etched on my mind and in my heart: the day when I committed my life wholly to Jesus. I couldn't know that day (nor could even the wisest at that service) what God had in store for a seven-year-old boy named Dino. But it was then, in that moment when I made that once-and-for-all decision, when I took that simple approach of saying, "Dear Jesus, take my life and my talents," that the life which God had intended for me to have, really began. I believe this with all my heart.

That simple yet profound step of asking Jesus to come into my heart—take my life, my talents, and use them—marked the beginning of all of God's workings in my life to this very day. That's when things really began to take place.

Later, when I could understand such things, I was to learn the significance to my family, especially my mom and my grandmother, of this early, definite commitment of my life to Jesus.

Why was it so significant, so fraught with meaning, so exciting and fulfilling for them—so laden with possibilities of the miraculous in my life in the days and years ahead? Just a child going forward in an afternoon meeting!

To my mother and my grandmother, this was something they must have expected, something they had been waiting for. It was the first sign to them of the fulfillment of the promise God had given them even before I was born! It was a confirmation, a seal that God was working in my heart through His Holy Spirit; that they would not have to wait till I was grown up before they could see God's hand on my life.

Why did this have such profound meaning for them?

Why? For the ultimate reason—my mother had been told by the medical authorities that her second child (me!) would be a stillborn baby—that I could not possibly be born alive.

That was the first miracle of my life, that I ever breathed the breath of life!

Greater still was the miracle of my *second birth* that Sunday afternoon. I've experienced much that is miraculous during my life. But nothing greater, nothing more spectacular, nothing more miraculous will ever happen to me, however long I live. So that experience as a boy of seven stands out like a beacon light.

Then, as I look back, I'm so grateful to the Lord for the fact that He let me be raised in such a solid church as Glad Tidings, where the leadership was one of discipline. Oh, there were times when I rebelled a bit. I didn't always appreciate the strict codes, the clear-cut distinctions between what a Christian young person does and does not do. Sometimes, when I mention that I knew what it was to have feelings of rebellion as I was growing up in an uncompromising church, people want to know what form my particular rebellion took. Well, thinking back, I can see it was mostly that I resented the prohibition against having anything to do with the performing arts. *After all,* I reasoned, *I was in the arts* —and it seemed incongruous to me that my church and my family and my Christian friends frowned on what to me were cultural pursuits as well as pleasure.

But I am thankful now for this firm refusal to compromise on the part of those to whom I looked for leadership in my life. For it's been this very thing—this stance for what we believe to be God's will—that has given me the spiritual foundation I have today. Sometimes I feel sorry for Christian kids who are permitted to make all their own choices and determine their own standards. And I'm glad for the discipline that shaped my thinking along those lines. This discipline was molding my life and strongly affects me even today. And when the time comes that certain choices have to be made, all that I've learned and absorbed—all that input of godly example and instruction that had been programmed into young Dino's impressionable mind—was and is a powerful factor in my making the right choices.

I thank God for the background He gave me. And there was so much joy and love in it all! Life was rich and full and there were never enough days and evenings to do all the things our church

provided for the children and young people. Too much religion? *Never.*

Christ has more than satisfied me. He has made life exciting and fruitful and fulfilling. And the end is not yet here!

But that is how it all began for me.

2
Meet the World's Finest Mother

Sometimes I stop and reflect on where I might be, and what I might be doing if my mother were not the person she is. At such times I wish I were a poet as well as a pianist.

Some lines written by Catherine Miles are particularly applicable to my mother, in her total dedication to her children:

> Whenever you hear of a man doing a great thing, you may be sure that behind it somewhere is a great background. It may be a mother's training, a father's example, a teacher's influence, or an intense experience of his own, but it has to be there or else the great achievement does not come, no matter how favorable the opportunity.

I could never discount the "intense [spiritual] experience" that was mine; but neither can I ever forget that it was my mother who provided the opportunities that first came my way. The greatest of these were the spiritual opportunities that were mine while I was still so very young. People are seeing more clearly than before just how important this is. Dr. Benjamin Spock, for example, writing for the *Chicago Daily News*, stated:

> Children under six get their concept of God directly from their parents. I envy the parents who see God clearly and

concretely, because they can then explain Him in a way that is easy for a child to understand.

This child psychologist would certainly envy my mother, for she unquestionably *sees God clearly and concretely.* But Mother would be the first to admit that this had not always been so. I'll let her give her own testimony, which she delights in sharing.

> My parents came from the island of Crete, Greece, and I was born in Hanna, Wyoming. We were not a Christian family, but we had many interests in the Arts: sculpture, architecture, music, and Greek folk dancing. There was a lot to keep us all busy.
>
> My husband (also from Crete) and I were married in New York City where we had met. At that time, 1937, a friend of ours had come to know the Lord Jesus Christ as his Saviour and was eagerly witnessing to us. My husband made a profession of faith but somehow didn't go on with the Lord at that time. One of my sisters was converted, however, and then she felt the call to work as an evangelist among our Greek people. I thought: *I'll wait and see if my mother accepts Christ, and if she does, then I will, too.* In the meantime, our first baby was born and we called her Christine, after my mother. It was about four years later that my mother was saved and filled with the Holy Spirit. I had still not accepted Jesus as my Saviour, but shortly afterwards, I did.
>
> Now the hope and desire of every Greek family is to have a son, so when I knew another baby was on the way I was overjoyed, and now I could pray and ask God to give us a baby boy. But in the third month of my pregnancy, complications set in, due to a fall I had. When the doctor told me I would lose this baby, I was nearly frantic: hadn't we waited four years —and now *this!* I did as the doctor said and stayed in bed. But

by now, my mother was on fire for God. I phoned her and told her the sad news. "Hold on, my dear child," she said over the phone, "I'll be right there and we'll pray. We have a big God and He is able to save that baby and use it for His glory." (I remember as though it was yesterday!) Mother came and she knelt down by my bed and prayed most of the night. Together we asked God to spare the child and to use it, whether a boy or a girl, to glorify Him. I fell asleep after a while. To this day, my mother does not know whether she was asleep or awake; whether she had a dream or saw a vision. But this is what she experienced: A big, black figure had me, holding me tightly around the waist and bouncing me about. When my mother saw what was happening, she yelled out, "Leave my daughter alone. She is washed in the blood of Jesus." Three times my mother repeated, "In the Name of Jesus, *let her go.*"

Her prayer was effective, and the figure—devil or demon or apparition—fled down the apartment stairs and out into the night. When Mother described it all to me, I realized that Satan knew all along that I had dedicated first my little girl and now this unborn child to the Lord, and the devil was trying to destroy the child even before he was born. But, praise God, *He* got the victory, and when my baby was born, to my unspeakable joy, the Lord had given us a boy.

Although I was just a new Christian I felt it was my responsibility to lead my children to Christ. And, since my husband was not living for the Lord in those days, I had to make a decision: should I go his way with him, or should I consider my children and raise them for Christ? This was no easy decision, for my own inclinations were still toward the things that had made up my own background. I would have to give up certain things such as our music and dancing which I really loved. Nevertheless, the Lord was with me and helped me make the decision. My children were not old enough to know right from wrong; my husband was—so the children needed me the most. My husband was old enough to make his own decision as to whether he would follow the Lord; the children needed my guidance.

In a very special way, the Lord rewarded me even in the days when my children were quite young. I can remember Dino coming and with his serious eyes looking right into mine saying, *"I've got something in me, Ma. I feel it."*

From his earliest days, Dino, his sister, and I never missed a church service. I hear people say sometimes, "Don't give a child too much religion. You'll just turn him against God and the church. I don't believe it. Children brought up in the right kind of church where Jesus is held up and you can feel the power of the Holy Spirit of God in every service—such children love every bit of it.

We were a very close family, and as Mother said, my sister and I were happy growing up in our church. It would have been wonderful to have had my father with us in heart and spirit, enjoying the presence of the Lord in his life. But God is faithful; we kept on praying for my father and God knew that the day would come when Dad, too, would be loving and serving Him.

People sometimes ask my mother about how she found out I had some talent on the piano. Her story never varies:

We had just come home from church, and my daughter and I had gone into the bedroom to take our coats off. Suddenly I could hear, coming from the living room, the notes of "At the Cross, at the Cross."

Who could be playing the piano? I tiptoed into the living

room. Sure enough. There was no one there but three-year-old Dino! I asked him, "Did you play that hymn just now?"

"Yes, Mama, I played it," he answered.

"Play it again," I said. And he did, using his thumb and pinkie. I couldn't believe it. Every note was perfect. And right then the Holy Spirit spoke to my heart, saying, "Remember the promises you made?" I looked up and answered, "Yes, Lord. He is Yours. Use him in a mighty way."

How I thank God that He permitted me to be born to a Christian mother. I'm thankful, also, that she is a faithful giver; that, having made her covenant with God in dedicating me to Him for His service, she never reneged, never squirmed out of it. The temptation was strong, for, as she has shared with me, other people pressured her to steer me into different, worldly channels. Even the members of her own family—successful in their professions—saw what they called "religious music" as a dead-end street.

"Train the boy for the day we're living in," they would advise. "Who wants to be bothered with religion?"

But Mother was firm as a rock. "When Dino is old enough, he can make his own choice," she would tell them, "but for now, he's going to church. He's going to use his talent for God."

There were some who noticed my playing and began to pester Mother to "put your son on TV and make some money"—sometimes it was a radio show. But Mother was adamant that she would not make money off her child. Not that we didn't need the money. In fact, when the time came for me to have lessons, Mother worked outside the home to provide the extra funds we needed.

She had another problem. Unlike many mothers, my mother didn't have to coax or cajole me into practicing the piano. The very opposite was true. I loved to play, even when I played the same piece over and over, my "At the Cross" number, nearly driving the neighbors crazy. As anyone who has lived in a New York City apartment building can testify, what one person does is very much the business of the neighbors. One man in the building threatened to take my parents to court.

"Enough is enough," he grumbled. "What's the matter with your kid? Why doesn't he go out and play ball or something, like other kids? When I want a little extra sleep in the morning, the boy's banging on that piano [I hope *banging* was a prejudiced opinion] and when I want to go to bed, he's at it again. Why doesn't he ever give up?"

A woman likewise complained very frequently. I'm sure these were not people who objected to music, or to piano playing in particular; they just wanted a few hours of peace, of respite from me and my practicing.

In the case of the woman to whom I referred, a nice thing happened later. A couple of years ago, she was visiting friends in Southern California and one of them said, "How would you like to go to a concert while you're here? I have tickets" (and she made the arrangements with this lady from New York City for them to attend the concert together). Imagine the surprise when onto the stage walked none other than the kid, now grown up, who had plagued this woman in her apartment in New York! It was a gratifying sequel.

She came and talked with me after the concert. We had a nice time reminiscing—and she forgave me completely for disturbing the peace. But, at the time, it was my mother who had to bear the brunt of the neighbors' displeasure. She put up with a lot in my pursuit of music. She tells that I picked up every piece I ever heard. If we were riding a city bus and along the way we heard some music, I would tap it out on the back of the bus seat; or, in a restaurant, I would drum a tune on the table.

Not only my mother, but also my grandmother, prayed big prayers: they really believed that God had a very special ministry for me.

Meet the World's Finest Mother

There was one thing very special about my mother, as far as my playing was concerned. She took it seriously. Some parents, delighted that their child shows signs of unusual ability on an instrument, regard this as "cute"—that's all. They're satisfied to have the child perform for friends and relatives (whether he wants to, or not) without providing either the incentive or the opportunity for him to develop any talent that he has. My mother is cut from different cloth. In the first place, she never forgot her covenant with God. It was this awareness that caused her to be sensitive to the voice of the Holy Spirit that day when she heard her three-year-old finger out "At the Cross." I'm sure my mother would have been equally sensitive if either of her children had shown unusual ability in another area. She had no idea what God's plans were for my life. She couldn't know what her part would be when God chose to take her up on her offer of her children for His service. But, without this constant sensitivity, she might have missed.

There must be thousands of children whose Christian parents, in all sincerity, dedicate them to the Lord. My mother went an extra step. She listened to the voice of God. And the day she first heard me play there was born the resolve that, whatever it cost her personally, she would provide the opportunities I needed.

What if she had not recognized that milestone in my life or, recognizing it, she had just hugged to herself the knowledge that she had a specially endowed child? What if—I wonder!

Another thing for which I can never cease to thank my mother is that, with all her intense enthusiasm and her high aspirations for me to sharpen this tool the Lord had given me, she never for one instant permitted my music to interfere with my spiritual development. Both Mom and my sister Christine could have so focused on my precocious performance that this could have tended to make me a pompous, obnoxious, bratty kid. Mom could have caused me to grow up feeling that my ten fingers were more important than my eternal soul or a life lived for God. But she didn't! God not only gave me talent: He blessed me with a wonderful family. You should meet my grandmother! She's something else. But that's for another chapter.

My family's great expectations for me have had a tremendous effect on my life. Perhaps some people might reason, "What right does one person, even a mother or a grandmother, have to commit a child to God?"—in the way my mother and grandmother did? What right? The right of love. The right of spiritual concern. And they asked nothing for me but the very best that can happen to a human being, that I might live my life in the center of God's will.

Much has been written about mothers. I like the simplicity of the tribute paid by a president of the United States, John Quincy Adams, to his mother: "All that I am my mother made me."

I say *Amen* to that.

3
The First Girl in My Life

> Family ties are precious things
> Woven through the years
> Of memories of togetherness . . .
> Of laughter, love and tears
>
> AUTHOR UNKNOWN

If you want the truth about a person, ask someone who has lived close to that person for a number of years. There were just the two of us children in our family, and, since my sister Christine is four years older than I am, she had to put up with her kid brother day in, day out, right until she left home to go to Bible college. So no *Dino Story* would be even half complete without her part in it. I've asked Chris just to "tell it like it was."

Where do you begin—what do you tell, and not tell—when it's your own brother you're writing about? And you know that thousands of people are going to read it!

As soon as some people learn that I'm Dino's sister, they begin to ask certain questions:

What was it like growing up with a brother like Dino?
Did you ever feel left out, since he had so much talent?

Did your parents favor him over you?

Was Dino this—and was Dino that? Was he fun to be with?

Most of the questions I've been asked had never been in my own mind; they would never have occurred to me. But since they are asked, I'll try to share with you something of what our life as children and young people growing up in the same home was really like. Actually, except for the fact that we were Christians and a lot of our life was wrapped up in our church, we lived pretty much like the rest of the people in our neighborhood in New York City.

As to my feeling left out, no, I never felt that. We were treated alike. What we did, we did together. I had the same opportunity that he had to take piano lessons. Dino played beautifully and I always enjoyed his talent. I did a little singing and he would play for me; then we sometimes sang duets with Dino taking the soprano (until his voice changed) and I, the alto.

I'm so glad that I never had any negative feelings about myself due to what my brother was. We were close. We loved each other; we still do. And my talents lie in just the right direction for me. I love being just who and what I am, a wife and mother—a homemaker. I enjoy doing things with and for my husband, Paul, and our five wonderful children. And Dino still has a place in my life. He likes nice things, a home that's neat and attractive, and he enjoys my cooking. So he often shares our home with us.

But back to Dino's talent. Mom and Dad and I felt he was fantastic—but that was just our family pride in him. We encouraged him to play because his music was so beautiful, not because we thought he was a genius.

I've also been asked if, as we grew up, I had the feeling that God had something very special for my brother to do for Him. I think I did, though I may not have expressed it. I knew Dino was in God's will; that was his own primary concern as far as I could judge. Of course, only God knows our hearts. I did feel that

The First Girl in My Life

a talent like Dino's wouldn't just go to waste, that if he kept close to the Lord, He would use my brother. But this sense of mission for Dino was not something that pressed in on us every day; it wasn't something we had to keep in mind and strive for. It could be that my mother and grandmother had this sense to a stronger degree, because of the circumstances of Dino's birth. But, for me, as a young person, God's leading in Dino's life just came about in its own time. (I don't know how he feels about this.)

I did know that his talent was not, in itself, enough. Because we went together for our music lessons and I was in the studio when Miss Smith was working with him, I knew that Dino had a hard time reading the notes. And reading the notes was all-important to our teacher. She really worked with Dino, but it was so easy for him to play by ear. He just had to hear Miss Smith play a piece once and he'd pick it up and play it—always in the key of C. But Miss Smith persisted and succeeded in making my brother understand the importance of being able to read the music and to play in every key.

Another thing we did together was to attend Greek school. We spoke Greek most of the time at home, because Daddy was more at home in his own language. But we couldn't read or write Greek, so we went to school to learn that. Classes were held in our regular school—P.S. 94—after school hours. There, too, we sang. We were used to singing and we volunteered our services. All we knew were hymns and choruses—never a popular song! We sang duets and I suppose the teacher thought it was cute for a brother and sister to harmonize together, so she kept asking us and we were only too glad to oblige.

We didn't stick exclusively to Manhattan for our singing performances. Oh, no! Mom had relatives on the West Coast that she liked to visit. So she would work extra and save for these trips. It was just the three of us, however. But, let me say, my father never hindered us; he never seemed to mind that the three of us were so close and that we did everything together. I think it pleased him that we enjoyed each other so much. Dear Daddy. I hope he knew how much we would like to have had him with us all the time.

Because there wasn't much money, we traveled on either the Greyhound or the Continental Trailways bus across the country. Our favorite seat was always in the very front, near the driver. There we could enjoy the wide sweep of windows and see everything there was to be seen. It was all so fascinating.

But also—and I don't know if this says we were very bold or just very stupid—we *sang*. Mom would whisper after we'd been going a little while, "Sing some hymns." So Dino and I would get our heads together, then we would start, softly at first, then before we knew it we were singing so loud the whole bus could hear us—and they loved it! Here we were, two bold little Greek kids singing hymns we learned in church and Sunday school. We could see the driver wink into the mirror, and everyone was laughing and smiling. All it took was for us to see the winks and the smiles, and we sang all the more.

Those were the days! That was fun.

Our introduction to handcrafts and games such as Ping-Pong was at a Neighborhood House for underprivileged children, just round the corner from our apartment. There were also opportunities for taking music lessons at a very low rate. I was quite young and had given up on my piano lessons from lack of interest. Mom let me start violin lessons, but that didn't last long either. We couldn't go often, but once in a while we were allowed to go to this Community Center.

A perpetual treat for us was riding the double-deck bus. We would get on and sit up top and drink in the fresh air. Our favorite ride was along Riverside Drive. It was so beautiful in those days. We would ride away uptown into streets in the 100s. Mom took us to Central Park whenever she had time, and—one time, leave it to Dino to fall off the slide and break his arm!

I still get chills when I remember one thing we did. It was my

The First Girl in My Life

doing, that time. The two of us went to a bicycle shop and each rented a bike. Mind you, neither of us had ever been on a bike! I wonder now why the owner didn't ask us if we could ride. He didn't! And off we went into the busy street traffic: cars, trucks, buses, taxis. If ever the Lord had His eyes on two foolish children it was that day! For we had not been going very long until I just escaped being run over by a car. That was enough. We took the bicycles back to the shop. Mom didn't find out about this escapade, but she might as well have, for I felt so guilty. Here I was, trusted to look after my young brother—and I might have had us both killed.

Ours were simple pleasures. We played a lot of hopscotch on the sidewalk. And, like most kids in the crowded sections of New York City, we got a kick out of playing in the spray from the fire hydrants the boys turned on. This wasn't a very good thing to do, of course. But it wasn't vandalism in the way we see it today—this was practically a survival technique in the sweltering heat of the summer. This was off limits for Dino and me, but we went anyway and sometimes we got away with it.

The fire escape is another spot where city children spend a lot of time. We especially liked to sit out on the fire escape at Grandma's. There was always so much going on, so many people coming and going on Ninth Avenue.

By the time you finish reading this book you will be as convinced as we are that για-για (that's Greek for "grandmother") is just wonderful. We think so, and we were never happier than when we were with her. She still lives in the same apartment. In her block is a fish market, a bar and grill, and a fruit store. Just around the corner is a little shop that had a big place in our lives. This store sold shopping bags for three cents, so whenever we went to Grandmother's we would take whatever money we had and stock up on these bags. Then we would go out on the avenue and shout, "Shopping bags, shopping bags—five cents." When we sold out our stock, we would go and buy more, line up both arms with the shopping bags, then go out again and sell them. There were other little kids doing the same. It was a great business—and almost clear profit! We had great fun and we were always looking forward to the shopping-bag days. There was a little candy store around the corner, where we spent our profits.

One thing about Dino: he could manage to get lost no matter where we went. We made a point of locating the Lost and Found at places like Coney Island, Macy's, and so on—for we were pretty sure we'd end up searching for Dino. And we laugh now (though it was not so funny at the time) about the night he didn't get off the bus when Mom and I did. It was a cold, snowy night—too cold for us to walk as we usually did—so we took the bus, and at our stop Mom and I were starting toward our house when I exclaimed, "Ma! Dino's still on the bus." As it started up, we could see him, slumped over the seat with his new little red earmuffs and all—and he was sound asleep! We ran after that bus, frantically trying to get the driver's attention. Finally he must have caught sight of me (I was a little faster than Mom) and he probably had just noticed his young passenger, alone and asleep, and figured he belonged to us.

Some of these things could happen only to Dino, and we never let him forget them!

One of his lovely traits is that he is so generous. He just loves to give. But, when we were kids this sometimes backfired on me. I would spend whatever money I had, on nice little things for the house or for myself, and I thought Dino was a bit of a hoarder with his money. When it came time for birthdays or Mother's or Father's Day gifts, though, he always had money when sometimes I didn't. I would say to him, "Dino, I'll help you pick out the gift, then I'll put both of our names on it." He was little and I could talk him into doing this. But then he would let the cat out of the bag: "It was my money; Chris just put her name on it," he'd say. But the *giving* was typical of him to this day.

I remember the time Mom said she liked a particular set of

The First Girl in My Life

dishes. Well, Dino decided he would get them for her for a special surprise. So he bought them, a dish at a time. I can see him yet; week after week, his hands clutching the package behind his back as he slipped into his room to stack the dishes under the bed. I knew all about it. And naturally Mom found out, too, as she mopped the floor under the bed. But she was properly "surprised" when, with great eagerness, Dino presented her with the set of dishes she had said she liked.

One of our trials—Mom's and mine—was that Dino was forever bringing home stray cats and dogs—and they were always pregnant. Daddy loved animals so he was always game to keep whatever Dino dragged home. I remember once it was chickens—little chicks left over from Easter in a store. But a chicken coop and sawdust in that apartment! Mom and I were glad when, one by one, the poor little things died. Then there was the time he got a bird (I forget if it was a canary or a parakeet) and he wanted it to have babies, in the worst way. He went to a pet shop and bought a hatching something or other. That was when Daddy decided he would play a joke on Dino, who was too young to be concerned about the biological necessity of having both male and female in order to raise baby birds. So my father put a grape in the bird cage and when Dino saw it, he was overjoyed. The bird had laid an egg! There would be a baby bird! It was the longest time before he realized that Daddy had fooled him.

Because Dad had his restaurant and Mom worked, it was my responsibility to look after Dino—and was he active! Now, I loved my brother dearly, but I wanted to be with my own friends who were my age. So I had to take him along. He was such a tease that he would get into trouble, then I would have to fight his battles for him. It wasn't any great big thing, but one thing after another. Sometimes I hated it. He was *always* around.

And that piano. Much as I admired his playing, sometimes in sheer frustration I would yell at him, "Dino, will you *please* stop playing that piano. Can't I have some peace and quiet?" There was never any privacy in those "railroad" apartments. One room opens into another and any sound is heard everywhere. Moreover, the neighbors screamed at us about Dino's constant practicing. Mom never had to make him practice, like most mothers have to. The problem was to get him to stop!

Young brothers do all kinds of things, I learned. One of the things we kid Dino about was his getting into my love letters from Paul. I'm fortunate in having a husband who is a beautiful writer; he can describe things so that you feel you are right there. When he would write to me, there was so much beauty in the letters, in the way he expressed his love for me! And when Dino was just beginning to be interested in girls, he would copy bits from Paul's letters. But they would be pieces describing the beauties of nature, the streams, and the mountains—and there Dino was, in the heart of Manhattan! What must the girl have thought when she received such a letter?

What did we city kids know about the beauties of nature? We didn't even appreciate it. Sometimes we would go to camp in the country and we could hardly wait to get home. It was so dark without the streetlights, and we weren't used to the quiet. But young Dino must have thought that Paul's descriptions made wonderful material for letters.

We didn't get away with much, as children, and the room arrangement in our apartment was no help. Mom believed in firm discipline—with no back talk (which she always seemed to overhear). For example, sometimes Dino and I would be allowed to go by ourselves to a young-people's activity at the church, with strict injunction to be home by a certain time. And let me interject that Daddy often was waiting at the bus stop to walk us home. Well, the meeting might be a bit late, or we would have a prayer meeting afterwards, or perhaps we were just enjoying the fellowship of our church friends and the time would get away from us. Well, did we get it from Mom for being late! This caused us to be rebellious. And I think it was a good rebellion, if such a thing can be. There are always things young people do, about which they feel their parents just don't understand. And Mom was always sure to hear us griping, and she punished us for that, too.

Mom was always fair (according to her rules). If she was sure which of us was at fault, that's the one she punished. And when we blamed each other—"It was her, Ma!" or "I didn't do it, it was him"—she had her way of dealing with our buck-passing. We *both* got the licking. But Mom was sure to hear us complaining, "She shouldn't have . . ." and she would stalk into the bedroom where we had gone to grumble, and ask, "Who is *she* you're both muttering about?" and with a slap she would say, "Now get to bed!" or "Sit quiet and *think about this.*"

Our mother was thorough about everything and I can now appreciate her discipline more than I did at the time—she knows that a child who is not taught to obey its parents will have a difficult time learning to obey God. With the discipline we never doubted Mom's love for us. She was—and is—a wonderful person, the finest of mothers.

How often we wished that Daddy was with us in spirit. But we appreciated him as a good father. We did so want him to enjoy the good things of the Lord, however, as the other three of us did. Sometimes Dad would walk with us to church (he's a great walker) and we felt the day would surely come when he would take his place with us in church.

We all walked a lot and we loved window-shopping. There's no place like New York City for window-shopping, especially at Christmas. Since our church was located right near the big stores —Macy's and Gimbels and others—what fun we had! (Half of our time was spent going and coming to church, *very happily,* let me say.)

I recall that we didn't always have to be *buying.* We could be happy just enjoying the fascinating windows or running in and out of the department stores at Christmas. There was so much excitement in the air—and the Salvation Army with the cheerful little ringing bell and the band playing. We loved to drop our offering into the kettle. We enjoyed everything—just looking at things, just being a part of the crowds in the crisp, cold air, and the snow that had turned to slush underfoot.

For us, Christmas Day meant a wonderful family gathering at Grandma's. (Everything revolved around Grandma, sort of like the Italian godfather.) There was the greeting of relatives and Dino and I were always first at the door with our "Happy Christmas" in Greek: Καλά Χριστούγεννα. There was the feasting on Greek dishes that we all loved, and the joyous fellowship with one another. We didn't have a Christmas tree in our home (only once do I remember us having one), but we didn't feel deprived; we didn't know "everybody" had a tree at Christmas.

It's a nostalgic experience looking back on those growing-up years. I remember them as very special. Dino and I had a wonderful life. They were very hard times, but my mother never let us know that they were hard times. Depression or no, she treated us as if they were *good times.* Yet, when I was a baby she even had to pawn some of her things—jewelry and stuff—to buy milk for me. But Mama always put her best foot forward. When we went to church, she could have been the wife of a millionaire. She had a flair for making the most of things, and she really knew how to dress. Mom always saw to it that we children looked our best, also.

In those Depression days we even had to use coupons to buy food. But it was just a game for me when Mama gave me some coupons to go to the neighborhood store and buy sugar. Not until much later did we learn how poor we really were (just like all our neighbors and millions of other Americans). Never once did Mama let us be aware that we were living through a Depression. She gave us everything, *and we took it.* It didn't occur to us until years later that she must have wanted some things for herself, but she put us kids first. The day was to come when she would be repaid, in part at least, for her unselfishness and loving sacrifice. But she couldn't know that. She just gave herself to us.

The First Girl in My Life

Another thing Dino and I never missed was what the world calls "pleasures." We had a full and happy life. Oh, there may have been times when, because he was in the Arts, Dino would have enjoyed some of the cultural pursuits that New York City is so rich in, but I'm sure he'll tell you his own thinking along that line. Sufficient to say, we felt *rich*. We enjoyed the security of loving parents, and the warmth and fellowship and joy of a spiritual church. We lived with the sense that Jesus Christ was at the center of not only each day but of our future. We could trust ourselves to His direction.

What more could Dino and I, his sister, have asked for? . . . Not a thing!

4
Thank God for Miss Smith

Recently, while I was in New York City, I paid a call on my first music teacher, Miss Florence Smith, in her attractive studio in Manhattan. For me—and as I discovered, for Miss Smith—this was a nostalgic time. If time had permitted I think I would like to have walked the city blocks from my childhood home, recalling each step of those weekly pilgrimages for my piano lesson.

I've heard it said that a teacher is many things. This certainly applies to Miss Florence Smith, the gracious lady who was my first teacher. She was and is a friend to all her pupils, and she has solid convictions as to what is good for children, even though she herself never married.

"A child must be loved for himself, apart from his performance," is her philosophy. No doubt she has in mind the "approval" that some parents give only when their child gets gold stars, rarely showing the same acceptance when their child's performance does not rate a reward.

Miss Smith gave us, her pupils, more than music lessons; she gave herself. And she has much to give. Unusually well taught by such masters as Arthur Friedman and Harry Rochelle, she has, in addition, the God-given ability to impart what she knows. She makes no bones about this. "Teaching is what God has given me to do," she states unequivocally, "and I know I'm a good teacher. When I meet one of my former pupils I can always have a good

Thank God for Miss Smith

feeling because I know I've done well by him or her."

How was I so fortunate to have such a fine teacher to start me on my musical adventure with God? Well, Miss Smith was a member of our church so we knew her in that capacity. She didn't play for our church services, however. I've heard her explain that her sister had played hymns so constantly that hymn playing was almost distasteful to her. Also, she feels strongly that her pupils, both Christians and those who are not believers, need a solid classical background such as she herself had in her profession. And among her pupils was one of my aunts, my mother's sister Anne. Apparently one day my aunt said to Miss Smith, "You must take Dino. He's beginning to play by ear, with two fingers. And if he doesn't soon get some instruction, he will never be a musician in spite of his natural talent."

Well, Miss Smith didn't jump at the chance, I assure you.

"How old is he?" she parried. "I don't like to take anyone younger than eight."

"He's six years old," my aunt replied, and after some hesitation Miss Smith said, "I'll take him. He's in our church, after all, so I suppose I should make this exception with his age."

They were difficult days, financially, for our family. But my mother was adamant that not only I but also my sister would have the advantage of Miss Smith's teaching. So the three of us would trek the distance from 63rd Street to 113th Street, rain or shine. I would always stop and buy some flowers for Miss Smith. While we had our lessons Mom sat patiently crocheting or knitting. She never complained; in fact she went to work to make the lessons possible for us.

Miss Smith had a practice of giving gold stars not for perfection in playing our pieces, but for memorizing them. She still recalls how easy it was for me to memorize. "Dino's book was filled with gold stars," she relates. Then with mingled frustration and tolerance she adds, "but he couldn't read a note!" (I did fool her for a while, though!)

She found what many another music teacher has discovered,

that it's difficult to teach a person who can play by ear to read the notes. So it was Miss Smith's task to teach me a note at a time until I could read the music. She soon found that not only did I have a perfect ear for music, but that God had also endowed me with the natural gift of perfect pitch (for not always do these go together). How good God has been to me! It's gratifying for me to know that my teacher sensed, too, that I always played with *feeling.*

Sometimes Miss Smith is asked if I had voiced early aspirations to become a concert pianist. To which she replies, "No, not at all. Dino confided at one time that he wanted to be an architect, possibly because he has an uncle who is a prominent architect. Another uncle is a noted sculptor. I saw Dino as a boy from a very gifted family, a person who could probably succeed in a number of areas."

Personally, she had the feeling that I would grow up to be a missionary. I'm not sure what gave her this idea. I'm just glad that she did see this in me in those early years. She's generous in her praise, saying that I never gave her a hard time, that I was cooperative, and "never a clock-watcher."

As to my becoming a missionary—who is to say what a missionary is, except that the word means "a sent one"? I pray daily that, indeed, I will fulfill my teacher's expectations; that I *will* be God's person serving Him in the power of the Holy Spirit wherever He sends me; that through my God-given talent I will be a missionary. Miss Smith has had many gifted pupils through the years. She didn't see me as special, as any kind of genius. I'm so thankful that she did, apparently, see in me someone whom God could use.

I guess I must have eaten up her teaching for it wasn't long before she told my mother she was giving me a new book because I'd gone right through the first one. She's told people that I could learn as much in five minutes as some people could learn in five hours. Be that as it may, she was and is a terrific teacher and friend. She takes a special interest in each pupil, so much so that one mother said, "I would not care how much my daughter learns just as long as she can spend one hour a week with Miss Florence Smith."

The question has come to her—could my God-given ability have possibly been destroyed by training? "No way," Miss Smith declared. "There's no way that real talent can be destroyed. But it has to be developed through education and hard work. People who have natural ability need to work the most, to keep them studying even when it's something they don't like doing."

She points out one of the snares for the naturally talented person—that such a person tends to play selectively in only one or two keys. Playing by ear, he is limited in his performance because he is not at home with all the scales. So the formula, no matter how talented the person, if he aspires toward excellence, is persistence in reading the music, and concentrating on practice —practice—practice. And this just has to take a different kind of self-discipline for the person who can sit down and play the piano by ear. . . . So I praise the Lord for a teacher who had firm ideas of what makes a musician.

I mentioned earlier that I had visited Miss Smith in her New York City studio. I did not go alone on that unexpected visit. But not until we had greeted each other warmly did I step aside and usher in another visitor. I'll never forget the look on Miss Smith's face—the astonishment and delight—when she saw who was with me: *Miss Kathryn Kuhlman.* We had come together to see my old teacher. She had a young pupil there at the time and she asked him to play for us. It was like a replay of my own experience, as she told me that this pupil, Michael, had the same ear for music, the same perfect pitch with which God had blessed me. How we enjoyed sitting listening to him play, then spending happy moments with Miss Smith. Apparently our visit meant much to Miss Smith, also. I learned later that she was the center of attraction when, the Sunday following our visit, the pastor mentioned it from the pulpit and asked, "How would you all like to have Dino and Miss Kuhlman come to visit *you?*" So I'm pleased that this visit made her happy.

It was in connection with her pupil, Michael, that Miss Smith shared what was a new insight to me. Apparently she was seeing in Michael what she had seen in me years before but which I cannot recall having heard her discuss before this time. It's the matter of confidence and poise in a performer. She claims that the greatest natural gift is not the perfect ear or the perfect pitch; it is the ability not to be afraid of people, not to be afraid of the instrument, not to be afraid of oneself. "Some people are so fearful that they practically back away from the instrument," she says, "and this fear paralyzes not only their fingers but their mind, robbing them of their memory. They cannot approach the piano without being tense and apprehensive; this can be true of even the most skilled and highly trained performers."

I had never thought of this. I had just accepted any confidence and poise I might demonstrate as a matter of course, as a part of who I am. It took this insightful woman, skilled and experienced in the profession, a woman who has given her life to draw music out of other people, to point out to me how great is this God-given gift, this ability not to fear myself—or other people—when I play.

Now, daily, I add this to my *thank Yous* to the Lord. For well do I realize how important it is to have such a gift, to feel self-assured and confident. Never would I want this to become *over*confidence, *self*-assurance in the ultimate sense of the phrase. But I do want to be ever aware that God had blessed me with His assurance, His ability in me. As He lets me exercise it, I pray that it will result in the audience being at ease as they listen. For I know that the performer's state of mind can soon communicate itself to the listener.

I have heard concerning the great Enrico Caruso that he held the belief that there was in him a "big me" and a "little me" and that his audience would intuitively respond to whichever was mastering him. The story was told on a telecast by Dr. Norman

Vincent Peale that on an opening night at the Metropolitan Opera in New York City, stage fright had so gripped Caruso that his heart was beating violently and his throat felt constricted. Then, just before he was due to make his entrance, a stagehand heard Caruso say, "You 'little me'—get out of my way!" and the master tenor stepped onstage to the resounding *bravo*s of the capacity audience. He had somehow overcome the fright that would have spelled defeat for him and disappointment for his listeners.

It's not God's will that we should be less than our best for Him. It's my feeling that we need not be the victim of *little*ness; that, rather, the Scriptures teach: "I can do all things through Christ who strengthens me" (*see* Philippians 4:13). The ability to operate on this premise is itself a gift from God.

How thankful I am for Miss Smith's insight along this line, and for the fact that she shared it with me as she shared so many other things—this teacher whom God sent into my life and for whom I praise Him even today. With the ultimate good of her pupils at heart, she was quick to spot it when one's ego was showing too much. She was fair, but cautious with praise.

"Too much praise can spoil a performer," is her philosophy. "It can boomerang." And unquestionably she is right. For if we are applauded constantly and overmuch, this can tend toward complacency and a letdown in consistent practice.

One of the incidents I feel I must include illustrates her point. It must have been a rather pouty young Dino who complained to her, "They didn't let me play in church last Sunday, Miss Smith." But, far from commiserating with me, she pointed out that there were other pianists and they had been playing faithfully ever since the church (Glad Tidings) was started. "You'll get your turn," she explained (cold comfort to me at the time, no doubt). "Just make sure you keep working hard so that you will be ready for it."

I can look back and appreciate her balanced attitude. Sometimes this is the very antidote needed to counteract the loving but unobjective attitude of the family who views a child as a prodigy, if not a downright genius. Of this first piano teacher of mine I can only say a heartfelt "Thank God for Miss Smith."

As long as we live, we must keep on learning—or stagnate. What is true of life in general is especially true of the world of the performing arts. The artist must keep on improving or he will surely deteriorate; he never "arrives." Because this is self-evident, as a professional I must keep taking instruction—and I do.

There was another teacher who made a tremendous contribution to my life. Her name was Miss Leland Thompson; she was my instructor at Juilliard School of Music—a genius in her field who had so much to impart to a pupil. Imagine my delight, when I came to live in California, to learn that my teacher from Juilliard had also moved to the West Coast. So, whenever I could make it, I would drive the hour and a half to where she lived and get a lesson from her. What a teacher—and performer—she was!

I had such high regard for Miss Thompson that I virtually hung on every bit of instruction she gave me. I admit I was even a little bit scared of her. Just once she attended a performance of mine. I was really nervous knowing she was out there in the audience. I remember, however, that I dedicated a number to her, a song I had written entitled "Eternal Love."

She was a hard person to witness to. I prayed daily for her salvation, and the Lord answered my prayers. Even while this book was being written, Miss Thompson called for me to come to what proved to be her deathbed. She was suffering from terminal cancer and I was the only pupil she asked to see. That day I was privileged to lead this wonderful musical genius to Jesus Christ who *is* Eternal Love. Today she is in His presence.

Miss Thompson will not read these words, but I want to pay tribute to her since she meant so much in my life. We will meet again, for her name is written in another book—"the Lamb's Book of Life" (*see* Revelation 21:27).

5
Our Boy, Dino

I'm proud to be known at Glad Tidings Tabernacle as "our boy, Dino." It's an honor and I appreciate that they think of me in this way.

So many good things have come out of our church, so many have gone from it to serve the Lord—for Glad Tidings has always been a missionary church. It's a church that believes the Bible is God's unerring and changeless Word. We were taught the Bible and it was there I learned to know and understand God's Word. And it was there—that Sunday afternoon when I was just seven years old—that I gave my heart and my life and my talents to Jesus Christ for all time.

And now I want to introduce my pastor, the minister of Glad Tidings for many years, the Reverend Stanley Berg. He has meant so much in my life. Go ahead, Pastor!

When I think of Dino, I think first of the young boy growing up in our own church, Glad Tidings Tabernacle, here in New York City. He and his mother and sister were very faithful in attending the services and, even as very young people, Dino and Chris made a real contribution musically, especially in Youth Church and Sunday school. Their mother and grandmother are loyal believers who loved their church and loved to pray. In later years the father came to know the Lord and joined his family in attending church and in serving the Lord.

Dino and our eldest son, Ken, grew up together in the church and although their paths seldom paralleled in their younger days, they later became close buddies. After graduation from different colleges, both enlisted (those were the days of the draft) and were sent to Fort Dix, New Jersey for basic training together. (I'm tempted to expose a photo of Dino with his "basic" skinned haircut—quite a contrast from how he looks today!)

On their return from military service, the two teamed up in launching Dino's new concert-and-record-album ministry. They shared an apartment in California where, through my personal contact with Dave Wilkerson, I had been instrumental in arranging to have Dino perform in Dave's crusades and rallies in California. In fact, it was because of these contacts that Dino went to California. I had been from the very first, chairman of Teen Challenge, and consequently I was very close to Dave Wilkerson. Dave appreciated having Dino—and through this we were to see God's plans for "our boy" begin to unfold.

For some time both Ken and Dino worked for Miss Kathyrn Kuhlman, and Dino still plays for Miss Kuhlman's rallies and her telecasts.

I recall that while he was still very young he was asked to play for our Youth Church and he had to reach high to even find the keyboard. At special services in our church he would also amaze everyone with his developing talent, this gift that God had given him. Even in those days he did not identify with the modern type of playing, either for religious or nonsacred music. There really seemed to be a serious note in his nature, a sacred quality about his piano playing that made it different, that made one realize God had His hand upon Dino for a gifted ministry. Throughout his high school, college, and military-service years Dino maintained this dedication. Again and again he proved the value of having a God-given vision to accomplish a purpose and goal in life

Our Boy, Dino

—and to honor God. Many times he would discuss with me the musical trends of the day and the way in which youth was attracted to the top hits. I was glad I could encourage him to maintain a steady pace, keep true to his calling and not allow modern bents to sway him from his goal. His main objective was to prove that people, especially young people, could and would be attracted to wholesome music if they saw and heard it presented by talented and trained artists.

He set his goals high. He was out to prove personally, by the very nature of his own life, that there is far more to the field of music than the average young person of today could find "outside." I'm convinced he has made his point!

While he was a student at The King's College near New York City, Dino continued to be our own director of music at Glad Tidings. Here, another area of talent came to light, his evident ability as conductor, arranger, composer. He trained and conducted our church choir in some important concerts held at Town Hall and at Hunter College, always with excellent attendance. This new field presented both a challenge and a form of temptation to Dino, as he mixed his abilities in these other areas with his skill at the piano. As this diversified opportunity confronted him, we talked it over a number of times and it was to his original calling that he gave his first loyalty. The keyboard had top priority.

I feel something of a personal pride in being able to have had a part in helping this young genius in his formative years when he was making important decisions that were to vitally affect his whole future life and ministry. And he was always so willing to listen, to accept counsel and advice. I admired this trait, so apparent in him. There were times when he needed moral support: leading a church choir can pose problems as well as a challenge. And he always rose to whatever was required of him, never hesitated to give his best to God and to the church. Few young men I have known can measure up to the stature of Dino Kartsonakis in complete dedication to the task set before him. This opinion has been even more reinforced by a statement made recently by Dr. Robert Cook, president of The King's College:

> Two great forces were evident in Dino's life from the moment he first entered The King's College. One was his love for music; the other, his love for the Lord. As I look back on his college career, and the years during which he served as an instructor on our faculty, I cannot remember a time when his thinking and planning and decisions were not entirely subservient to these great concepts.
>
> This fact made for an early maturity. Dino did not seem to have to go through freshman fright, sophomore shakiness, junior jaundice, or senior sag. He always seemed to know what he was doing, where he was headed, and whom he was serving. His choice of repertoire, while technically brilliant, was always calculated to bring glory to the Lord Jesus Christ. King's is the richer for having known Dino Kartsonakis. His influence still is felt among us, and we pray for him earnestly, lovingly, and regularly.

A normal youth, he enjoyed friendship and the companionship of both sexes. Yet he never permitted even the nearest and dearest to detour him from his main objective. Oh, yes, he was at times misjudged and misunderstood. But unless one was close enough to him to realize the burning motivation and desire to please the Lord and achieve his own goals, such a critic would certainly miss the point entirely.

Like all of us, Dino has his imperfections. But it has been my experience with him that he would not hesitate to admit mistakes or wrongdoing when he realized he had erred. In fact, I have heard him say that *not* to do something when we see sin and shortcoming in our lives *is a very great sin for a Christian.*

His sense of humor has helped Dino overcome some embarrassing situations. For instance, mistaken for an Italian, he would play along acting out the part—until something of his true Greek personality came through and was recognized.

Not born to be an athlete, he nevertheless participated in sports activities when with his friends and sports was their interest. He could be the life of the party and was always much sought after as an asset to social gatherings.

I remember his first car, a small sports model, and how he tried (like the rest of us) to buck the New York City traffic. It may be that this is where he learned some early lessons in frustration tolerance and reaction. Many, like Dino, have been born and reared in the big city—in a teeming complex—and have later moved from it to a more livable and affluent setting. They may either forget or overlook the place they came from. Not so our boy, Dino. He is appreciative of his background and early environment. He's grateful to everyone who has contributed in any degree to what he is today. It's not unusual for him, when his travels bring him our way, to pop into a service. Not long ago he had just a few minutes, but he played for us and gave a word of testimony, then left and escorted his beloved grandmother home before heading for the airport.

We at Glad Tidings are proud to call Dino "our boy" and we unitedly rejoice that God is using him in such a rich service that blesses so many people.

It is true that parental influence has much to do with the training and focus of a child's future life. There was no exception in Dino's case. As we indicated earlier, he has a godly mother and a godly grandmother who influenced him tremendously. They brought him to church regularly—and I mean *regularly.* He didn't rebel at this. Oh, maybe sometimes there was a little rebellion or frustration, but that's typical of the young. He learned to reverence and honor the House of God. And I believe this built into him something in his very thinking, especially into his music —how we can express to God what is in our hearts through music. We greatly appreciated having had the whole family ("whole" after Dino's dad came to know the Lord). All of them were so faithful and dependable. The mother sang in our choir; sometimes she sang solos with her young son accompanying her. She herself has a great appreciation for music. It's my belief that there's something deeply important in a young life—the home atmosphere and the culture that is there. Dino has had the rich heritage of honoring God in his early life and of being encouraged in the area of his talent.

Now, with the others in the family all living in California, we still have Dino's grandmother. There she is, service after service, in her place in the same church pew where she has worshiped all these years. She is a tremendous force for God with her devoted life of prayer and witness right here in our church area.

Many times I have talked with Dino concerning his future. I'm so happy that he never hesitated in discussing these important matters with me. He still does when he is around, and sometimes he'll phone to talk about something that's on his heart and mind. We're indeed privileged to have had the opportunity of sharing just a little in the development of this life for God.

Only God knows—*and He does know*—what the future holds for Dino. But no matter where he may go, no matter to what heights God's will might take him, to us, the pastor and people of Glad Tidings Tabernacle who love him, he will always be "our boy, Dino."

6
Miracles — You Better Believe It!

I ponder my own life and woven into it I can trace an ongoing thread of the miraculous. It seems so fitting that I have the opportunity and privilege of being a part of a miracle ministry. And I'm convinced that God knew exactly what He was doing in bringing me together with Miss Kuhlman. For *I believe in miracles!* My own life (even before my birth) has been a miracle.

It's a misconception that miracles have to be spectacular. Not at all. Although some people don't seem to realize it, miracles are not always supposed to be dramatic and physical. To me, a miracle is God meeting some special need, doing something for me that I cannot do for myself. A miracle is the Holy Spirit using me to help meet someone else's need. Like—well, just this very day I met a person who really needed help. I'm sure it was the farthest thing from his mind that we should meet, that I would talk to him, and he would tell me of his great need. I spoke to him about Christ, told him of the hope he can have in Jesus. This, to me, is a miracle.

"It's coincidence," say many people who sluff off such miracles. But for the believer in Jesus there's no such thing as *coincidence.* The word just isn't in my vocabulary.

For instance, there was this young fellow we'll call Frank. His parents had witnessed to him and they were earnestly praying for him. But Frank kept pushing the other way, resisting the conviction of the Holy Spirit. Then one evening he agreed to attend one of my concerts. "Just because *I like piano,*" he told them. "I'm not going for anything else, so don't get any ideas."

It *happened* (if you believe in coincidences) that one of the pieces I played that night was "The Holy City." Now, although this guy professed not to want to have anything to do with Christ, or to appear interested in what his folks wanted for him, somewhere in his background the beautiful "Holy City" had touched his heart. And when I asked for requests (he told me this afterwards) he had planned to test me out by asking for this number —but didn't.

But the Lord knew Frank would be there, and the Holy Spirit led me to include "The Holy City" on that program.

Again, it *happened* that between numbers as I was sharing some of my own beliefs with the audience, I specifically talked about the fact that God has a plan for our lives and that things do not just *happen.* And this was what made Frank begin to consider that perhaps God had a plan for his life. That night he accepted Christ as his Saviour. Coincidence? No, it was one of God's miracles.

Miracles are all around us. I believe it! There's a new book by Pat Boone titled *A Miracle a Day Keeps the Devil Away.* That's something to think about.

Back to *coincidence:* how often when I've been seeking God's will in a specific matter, suddenly a chance encounter begins to jell things together and I find myself in the peace-filled center of God's will. I mean I can actually trace back how God has done this. Was it a coincidence that the only right contact had been made at the precisely right moment? No, it was a miracle. Actually, this has been the story of my life—God causing me to be in the right place at the right time with the right combination of people. Only God can do this consistently.

Especially when we are wholly committed to Jesus Christ, *coincidence* just isn't in the dictionary. There's a purpose, a reason for every move you make. I've grown to expect the miraculous. And I believe that God works in our lives according to the measure of our expectation. I wouldn't want to live without this excitement, this freshness.

It's a cycle of blessing: God blesses me—I recognize that it *is* God's hand on my life—I praise Him for it—I look expectantly for Him to bless me again in a particular way. And so the cycle goes. You never know what God is going to do for you next, when you have this expectant spirit.

The other day I heard of a man who expresses it this way: "I can't wait to get up in the morning and see what God's going to do today." I like that. It's how I feel about my walk with God. It's eager, challenging, joyous. And why not? Jesus promised us abundant life. *Abundant*—no skimpy measure, but all we can possibly contain of joy and peace and love: all the good things only He gives—for ourselves, and enough to spill over to other people.

And it's all tied in with our commitment to Him.

As I've already shared with you, I was just seven years old when I gave my heart to Jesus, totally: my life and the talents He has given me. And that's when things began to happen in my life.

Some people may say (or think, even if they don't say it) that a child is incapable of such commitment, that, "He doesn't know what he's doing." Oh, yes, he does. Yes, a child can have this experience. *I know.* People can question our *theories,* but they cannot deny our *experiences.* And for me, that Sunday afternoon in New York City, something new came into me. Now I believe it was none other than the Holy Spirit—the presence of God in the Person of the Holy Spirit.

The experience is as fresh in my mind today as it was when it happened. It was a miracle of God's grace. When the Holy Spirit comes into a life He exalts Jesus Christ.

We read in John 16:13, 14 that when the Holy Spirit is come He will not speak of Himself: *He will glorify Christ.* This is the hallmark of the work of the Holy Spirit. If I may say it reverently, this is the Holy Spirit's credentials. It's important for us to keep in mind what *is* the ministry of the Holy Spirit of God. He never takes away from Jesus—He enhances Him. He lifts up the Name and the Person of Jesus Christ. He places all focus and all sights on Jesus. We might say the Holy Spirit is out to promote Jesus!

I'm glad I knew this, that from my earliest days I knew it. If God was going to be able to use me, I had to keep this emphasis. I never plan a program or never give a concert without purposefully and intentionally choosing some numbers that particularly focus on the Lord Jesus Christ.

Even now, it comes to me with a rare sense of delight that the first—the very first—piece I ever played in my life was "At the Cross, at the Cross," a hymn that speaks of the death of Christ on the cross, for our sins.

Among my favorite songs is: "Jesus—Jesus—Jesus—There's something about that Name." (I can't begin to tell you what that does to me as I play it. I *can* tell you that it lifts me into the heavenlies with Him.)

Another favorite is "The Savior Is Waiting." This is *so true:* "Time after time He has waited for you. And now He is waiting again."

And a melody that haunts me often is: "He's the Savior of My Soul"—for Jesus *is* that to me. Nothing can so put people into the climate of really worshiping Jesus than these beautiful songs which glorify Him.

So, even at that early age, when the Holy Spirit flooded my being, the first thing I wanted to do was to exalt Jesus, to excel in my talent *only to exalt Him.* I wanted to represent Jesus in the very best way possible. I believe the Holy Spirit endues us with this enthusiasm to be our very best for Christ.

This is what happened to me at the age of seven.

The Holy Spirit knew I would be a more effective representative of Christ if the talent which God had given me was developed and sharpened. I feel that God—that the Holy Spirit—is very practical (and I don't mean to be sacrilegious about this). The Holy Spirit knows the world we live in. He knows the competition that surrounds us. He knew, way back on that day when I was seven, that out there in the world were great pianists: talented, accomplished performers. But He wanted to do something very special in my life. So, that very day, when I was seven years old, He placed the desire in me to be satisfied with nothing less than I could be with God's help. (Our neighbors didn't always appreciate my persistence!) I have never for one minute doubted that it was the Holy Spirit who instilled in me this urge—this compulsion to excel.

I felt it then and I feel it now today. I know in the depths of me that this was more than a desire for an ability to perform well and be on a professional par with the fine performers. The Holy Spirit knew that if He was *in* me and *with* me as I perform, that I would have so much more than the skill and polish of an accomplished concert pianist.

It's the Holy Spirit who gives this added dimension—that "magic" which the world talks about. Frequently, when worldly persons hear me play they exclaim, "There's a magic in your playing." That's the only way they can describe it. I know what it is! It's the miracle quality that the Holy Spirit's presence adds.

Yes, I believe in miracles.

I believe, too, that there is in everyone—in you—a talent and ability that God wants to use. And if you will only turn this over to Christ—make a simple commitment of yourself and your talents—you, too, can be a part and a partaker of God's miracle.

I never get over how simple and yet how profound it is. You know, sometimes I'm glad I'm not all that intellectual. So many intellectual people try to analyze and rationalize man's relationship with Christ and the place which the Holy Spirit has in our lives. And they miss it entirely. They get hung up on something they read, they trip over their intellect, and lose the simplicity of it all. If they could be as little children—as babes—*as I was!* I was so very young when it all happened. My simple commitment of my life to Christ was so simple and yet so profound. This has had a tremendous impact on my life. It has kept me in the center of God's will.

It is my firm belief that God is willing to reveal His plan for our lives. First, though, I need to tell you that I have this unshakable conviction that God does have a plan—an individual blueprint—for your life and mine, that He creates a precise, individual plan for each of His children. It would be unreasonable to think otherwise. Would the God who numbers the hairs of our head and who individualizes our fingerprints not have a plan and purpose for our whole life? That would be incongruous. It would be out of character for our heavenly Father. (Think of the plans which earthly parents have for their own children!)

However, I've learned that we have to *want* God's will. The Lord does not force His will upon anyone. This is the glory of the human race, that God has created us with a free will—even a will we can exercise to reject Him. Think of that! If ever I might be tempted from God's perfect will as He reveals it for my life, I think I would be haunted by some lines I once read:

> When I stand at the judgment seat of Christ,
>   And He shows me His plan for me,
> The plan of my life as it might have been
>   Had He had His way, and I see
> How I blocked Him here, and I checked Him there,
>   And I would not yield my will . . .
> Will there be grief in my Savior's eyes,
>   Grief, though He loves me still?
>
> AUTHOR UNKNOWN

That's so tragic—and so possible. We can, and many do, miss out on God's perfect will. But here again He demonstrates His grace toward us. It should encourage us that He will see us through with His second best, His permissive will, if we choose not to have His best or somehow miss out on it. As A.B. Simpson phrases it:

> God has His best things for the few
> That dare to stand the test;
> God has His second choice for those
> Who will not have His best.

For me, God's perfect will is that I serve Him through my music. I know this in the depths of my being. I have the peace about it that God promised we can know if we keep our minds stayed upon Him (see Isaiah 26:3).

Knowing and sensing that I am in God's perfect will, I can step out on the stage with the confidence and expectation that Jesus is right there with me. A person may say to me afterward something like this:

"Dino, I watched you as you played. You would look up as though you were seeing Someone the rest of us couldn't see at that moment. Then a quiet, jubilant smile would play over your face and your eyes would light up. It was almost as though you were aware that Someone was keeping His eyes on you as you played. It was as though you were *inspired* as your fingers flew over the keys."

There's a whole lot of insight in that evaluation of my playing. For that is exactly how I feel. I might never have articulated it in those words myself, but I *do* feel inspired. I feel empowered by the Holy Spirit as I play, and I wouldn't want to perform any other way. I can't explain it, but then if I could—it wouldn't be supernatural. It wouldn't be a miracle.

By *miracle*, here is what I mean with regard to my playing. I mean that the music itself will minister to people as they listen. I feel very strongly about this.

Let me make it very clear, however, that I would never minimize the effect that music has on the entire service. The right music can set just the climate, just the mood for people to be ready to hear and heed the spoken message. Music can somehow create that perfect atmosphere in which the Holy Spirit can work on hearts. I thank God for this.

But I believe there is more to music than its being a climate setter. There's a lot being said and written and there is much research being done in our day on *music therapy* as a medical technique. Good as this may be, the concept I have in mind goes far beyond such a theory. There's no reason why I cannot some day sit down and play the piano and people listening will be healed—both physically and spiritually. I believe this. I really do. And I want to be more than a skilled artist for God. My prayer is that the Holy Spirit will take my music and minister through it as only He can—and make people whole. Perhaps this is why I never tire of playing "He Touched Me and Made Me Whole."

I've never doubted that God is still working miracles. Let me share with you the one that perhaps more than any other physical miracle has indelibly impressed itself on my mind and my heart. It was at one of Miss Kuhlman's services. A young man seated way up in the third balcony, a person who had been blind from birth, suddenly was able to see. It was awesome. It was dramatic. He ran all the way down to the main floor and up on the stage. And I'll never forget the look on his face—a look of pure praise to God. And his words—"Holy, holy" and "Jesus."

I can never play that beautiful hymn "Holy, Holy, Lord God Almighty" without seeing in my mind's eye that young man for whom the Lord had performed a great miracle, and the recognition he gave to Jesus and to Almighty God.

Miracles—you better believe it!

Here I am with Mom, Dad, and Chris in a family portrait.

Four years old: New York City on Amsterdam Avenue, near Grandma's.

Chris and I with our two grandmothers—New York in mid 1940s. *Right:* Grandma's holding our baby cousin here.

All dressed up at eight years old. *Below:* With the quartet "Christian Keynotes" from Glad Tidings Tabernacle.

Piano music at luncheon in Germany for army officers' wives.

With Miss Kathryn Kuhlman, a great source of encouragement to me.

Recording session with David Rose for "The Miracle" album. *Below:* Reminiscing with old friend and Sunday-school teacher, Paul Dilena.

7
I Knew Dino When . . .

No one ever makes it on his own.
Many people have contributed to my life, one of them being Inspector Paul Dilena of the New York City Transit Police. He was my Sunday-school teacher at Glad Tidings Tabernacle, and if you have read *The Cross and the Switchblade* you recall his name. He was the police captain in the book, and now is treasurer of Teen Challenge.
In a way Mr. Dilena has been a part of my life since I was very young; in fact, he says he's known me since I was born, and to this day his family and ours are close friends.
But—should I let him tell everything he knows about me? I'll take a chance. Go ahead, Inspector, you're on!

Not long ago my wife, Sonja, my son Timothy, and I were visiting in Southern California and of course we spent some time with the Kartsonakis family at their home in Huntington Beach. On a Sunday night we attended one of Dino's concerts—and my mind flashed back over the years.
I remembered the little kid Dino who could pick out tunes, unerringly, with two fingers . . . the second-grader playing for Children's Church, and later soloing . . . the guy who was always willing to play for the Rescue Mission meetings, for programs to

I Knew Dino When . . .

cheer the elderly, and for retarded children . . . the budding genius who put as much of himself into playing "Jingle Bells" and "Santa Claus Is Coming to Town" when our church put on a program for underprivileged children in the city, as he did in his big concerts. . . . These, and a hundred other memories, crowded my mind that night.

With my wife sitting beside me at the concert and our son right ahead of us, I was reminded of another concert. Sonja sang in Dino's choir, and because she was expecting a baby any day, she begged off singing in that concert. Dino was disappointed. "Please, Sonja, I need you," he said, "and—tell you what—you sing for me, and when the baby's born I'll be his godfather!"

He was very persuasive. My wife did sing in that Saturday-night concert, our son Timothy was born the very next day, *and Dino is his godfather.*

When Dino began to be well known around New York, people would sometimes say to me, "You're Dino's Sunday-school teacher. Tell me, is he a good student?"

I don't know what they were hoping to hear, but I never fudged on my answer. "Not really," I'd tell them. "Dino's heart has always been in his music."

Dino himself tells this about those days in my teenage class at Glad Tidings:

> Mr. Dilena was always asking questions: Bible verses, chapters, and so on. He would look over the class and when he picked on me I would say, "Will you please repeat the question." Then when he did repeat it, I'd look him right in the eye and say, "I still don't know the answer."

We laugh over this now when we're together. And I guess that in the intervening years, Dino has learned a lot of those answers. I always found him cooperative. He could take discipline, he could take instruction. I suspect that these fine traits explain much of his excellence as a performer, and his good relationships with other people.

It's been exciting watching through the years, on the sidelines, as it were, while the Lord's plans have been unfolding in Dino's life. (I wonder where he would be today if he had not had this ongoing consciousness of the presence of God guiding him.) From his earliest days he appeared to sense that God's blessing on his life and his talents would come as he obeyed the Word of God, and never compromised his beliefs.

The military service is a known breeding ground of temptation, and for Dino this came in a subtle form. He was offered a promotion—something like stepping up several ranks all at once—but this involved taking over the band, which was a jazz band. Rather than do this, Dino turned down the promotion with all its benefits.

But God is faithful and He has said, "Them that honour me I will honour" (see 1 Samuel 2:30). The fantastic story of how God rewarded Dino in this decision is told in another chapter. Sufficient for me to say here that God knows how to honor the person who puts Him first. It always delighted me to realize that, in addition to making Dino a tremendous blessing to people who might otherwise never have heard him play, or have heard his testimony, God threw in a special bonus. For it was while in the army in Europe that Dino was able to study with some of the world's finest masters of music.

My recollections of Dino don't always come in chronological order, so you might find me wandering from one time span to another as I share these memories with you.

We were, understandably, very proud of the talented young pianist in our church. Every time he gained recognition it was as if our whole church family had scored points. There was the added interest that Miss Florence Smith who was Dino's first piano teacher was also a member of our church.

I Knew Dino When . . .

The Assemblies of God held talent-search contests and it was no contest for Dino—he always won top honors in his class. When he had won first place for the whole of New York State, he was eligible to represent the state in the Assemblies of God national contest. Glad Tidings very gladly sponsored his trip to the Gospel Publishing House in Springfield, Missouri. I think he was in high school at the time.

The piece he selected was "It Will Be Worth It All." As we had been sure he would, Dino won first place in this contest. He received a tremendous standing ovation. But there was more to this experience than success and applause. He looks back on that occasion as a spiritual milestone in his life. Here is what he told us when he returned from Springfield:

> It's kind of hard to explain what happened. While I was playing the hymn "It Will Be Worth It All" it was as if something—Someone—was gripping my fingers. I felt the power of the Spirit of God, and I could not move my hands just where I might want to. I could only move them where God wanted me to. And the people responded—oh, how they responded; they applauded; they wept; they were blessed. I never before realized that *music itself* could be anointed by the Holy Spirit—that He could take the notes and minister through them to people's hearts.

That was the beginning of a new power in Dino's playing and a new experience for the audiences who heard him play.

Because I've known Dino since the day he was born, some folks ask me, "Did you recognize early that here was an unusually gifted boy?"

I can honestly answer, "No question about it. No question at all." In fact, his own family recalls that I was the one who kept saying, "Dino's the greatest!" My wife, Sonja, has always felt the same. And you should hear her sister! She would come home from choir practice raving about "this young pianist who can play *anything*—and play it in any key."

One thing that stands out in my mind was that Dino was always willing to do whatever had to be done. This is not true of all artists. Dino would do some of the things these others considered beneath them as performers. I would say to him, often quite impatiently, "Dino, you shouldn't be doing this kind of thing. You're the *star*." (He never likes to have that word applied to him, even today.)

I remember getting quite impatient with him one night and I lectured him, "Let some of the others on the program do that. Why are you running around putting up risers, looking after the microphones, and all that sort of thing? Some of the others on the program won't lift a finger. They're all prima donnas!"

I didn't get far with my ranting. I had to go along with him as he kept right on doing those things that have to be done if the performance is going to be smooth and not amateurish. He had a much more Christlike spirit than I had about these things, I'm afraid. He could never see that he was any different, or that he should have any more special favors than the other fellow. He never forgot the *source* of his talent, or his relationship with Jesus Christ.

And, in the end, Dino was right and I knew it. Whether he wanted to be called a star or not, he was exactly that. The others just rode on his coattails. They just shared the program with a performer who wasn't too big in his own eyes to do the menial tasks.

I was the teacher. I was the one who should have been more aware and more mindful that God's Word teaches: ". . . he that humbleth himself shall be exalted" (Luke 14:11).

I saw this in Dino's life. He was willing to take the humble place—and God just kept raising him up to a higher place.

Another way in which Dino's fine spirit shows is that he can accompany other people and make them sound better than they are. There's that genius about him.

He didn't play for what he could get out of it financially. I remember what we laughingly called "honorariums": sometimes it was five dollars. (At Christmas, when he was very young, it was a bag of candy and maybe a stuffed toy.) Dino played because he liked to play. It was no secret that he was bringing pleasure to people, for they always let him know it by their smiles and applause. He was always willing to use his very great talent in something many considered too small for them to bother with.

I think I was a kind of buffer for him. I relaxed him, I hassled him and heckled him, and I put him at ease just by kidding around. He appreciated this. We had a wonderful relationship—we still do—not just Sunday-school teacher and pupil, but friends.

And sometimes, in my effort to do the right thing for him, I goofed. Here's the classic example we can laugh at now, but it wasn't funny at the time.

During the intermission at a concert in Carnegie Hall, some people wanted to see Dino. One person was quite insistent. But I told him what I'd told the others, "Dino's resting—he'll be coming out in a few minutes." The man wasn't one bit pleased that I wouldn't let him into Dino's dressing room.

I told Dino and he asked, "Who is he?"

"I don't know—I just chased him away," I answered.

Later, we learned that this was Dino's instructor from Juilliard—a noted teacher, and he had just wanted to encourage Dino and give him a few pointers! They got together afterwards, and it worked out all right. Sometimes we try too hard to do the right thing.

There was a very dramatic incident we shared. As I've indicated I felt there was nothing Dino couldn't do in his profession and once, when I was out on the West Coast, I had encouraged Ralph Wilkerson of Melodyland in Anaheim to get Dino to work with him. Then, when Dino came home from his tour with the army, he and his mother and father came over to our house. We talked about what Dino was going to do now that he was released from duty, and he told us he had an inviting offer to return to Europe to give concerts for a year. There was just one thing: it meant reenlisting. And he had only seven days to make this decision. So we phoned Ralph Wilkerson. I can remember every word of that conversation. It was brief.

"Let me think it over, Paul," he said.

I answered, "No! No thinking. It has to be yes or no—right now. Dino has just seven days to make up his mind"—and I told him about the Army offer.

It had seemed such a good idea. But it was evident later on that it was not *God's* idea; not His will for Dino. And apparently Ralph had some feeling that if he did take up this option, Dino might not stay with him very long, that Dino was "too big" for his work. But Dino himself has said, "It must not have been God's will, for I know that if I'd gone with Ralph Wilkerson I would have been very loyal to his ministry. I would have stayed with him, and this would have limited me; I could not have branched out." (Dino has since played a number of times for Ralph.)

I'll leave it to Dino to tell you how God worked things out for him that day.

There are two kinds of Christians: the ones who are afraid to go ahead with anything for fear they are "running ahead of God" and the others like me, who are sometimes guilty of not waiting for God's time.

I had thought how wonderful it would be for Miss Kuhlman to have someone as good as Dino on her program. In my book, the musician she had—well, it was no contest. Dino had it! I suggested this to someone else. But he was wise, and discouraged me at the time. God had the place and He had the

I Knew Dino When . . . 71

time for Miss Kuhlman to hear Dino play and make her own judgment. (She has shared that in her introduction to this book.)

I'm glad to have had a small part in Dino's life. As a Sunday-school teacher, I can honestly say it was a pleasure. As a law officer, I would like to say that we need more young people like him. Even when he was growing up as a teenager he never gave any trouble. As I've said earlier, he was always obedient. We can't always say this about even kids from Christian homes and boys and girls who themselves claim to be Christians. Dino would never violate the law.

There was something different about him. I see it as the result of his upbringing by his mother and his grandmother. (Every boy should have such a grandmother!) Also, he worked so hard for the Lord. With his talent and his sense that *God had given it to him*, he lived in this spiritual atmosphere. If he ever created any problems, I never knew of them.

To me he will always be the Dino who said, "Will you please repeat the question."

And now that Inspecter Dilena has said all these nice things about me, I want to share with you one of the greatest lessons he has taught me. It's this:

He had his own area of service for the Lord, both in our church and in the needy ministry of Teen Challenge. But Paul—and people like him—encourage other people. They allow God to use them to be a blessing. They give themselves—and while they're doing this *God is blessing them*. God was raising Paul to a responsible position in the police force. So, when you extend yourself to help others, God blesses you.

At Glad Tidings there was this spirit of always looking out for each other. We were concerned about each other's progress. It's when a person starts thinking only about himself and concentrating on his own affairs, that he begins to go down. I've seen this happen a lot of times. And there are some people who just can't handle success!

Through the years I've seen in this Sunday-school teacher of mine, a man whom God could bless and whom He could trust with success. My life is the richer for having him as a friend.

8
Everybody Should Have Such a Grandmother

How many lovely stories have been written about "going to Grandma's house"! For me, some of my very earliest memories are connected with my grandmother—για-για, we called her (which is Greek for *grandmother*).

Did you know that only one grandmother is mentioned by name in the Bible? That's right—*Lois*. And her chief claim to fame is because of her spiritual influence on her grandson Timothy (*see* 2 Timothy 1:5). He must have called his grandmother για-για for he too was Greek. Timothy's father was Greek (*see* Acts 16:1–3) and the fact that Timothy was not circumcized as a child would indicate that, although he had a Jewish mother (a believer) Timothy was brought up in an otherwise pagan Greek home. I know how fortunate he was, for I still remember sitting on my grandmother's lap—her name is Christina—as she talked to me about Jesus and prayed with me and told me Bible stories. I couldn't have been more favored in this respect if I had been the boy, Timothy, living in the first century A.D. For, like him, I have a godly mother and a godly grandmother.

It can also be said of me what Paul wrote to Timothy: ". . . from a child thou hast known the holy scriptures, which are able to make thee wise unto salvation through faith which is in Christ Jesus" (2 Timothy 3:15).

Nothing could be more true. The influence of my grandmother

—the spiritual atmosphere with which she surrounded me, her prayers, her total dedication to the Lord have done so much to mold my life.

To this day when I'm confronted with a problem or when I have to make a major decision, I get in touch with my grandmother and ask her to pray. I *count* on her prayers.

Let me make it clear that my grandmother's faith, magnificent though it is, could never have saved me. Salvation cannot be inherited; it cannot be willed to even the most beloved child or grandchild.

But my grandmother left no stone unturned in her faithful witness to my sister and me. In this she had the wholehearted cooperation of my mother, who also looked to Grandma as a tower of spiritual strength.

I'm sure that if I had ever been tempted to stray from the Lord, to wander into sinful paths, I wouldn't have had a chance. Not with my grandmother praying! Oh, I don't mean to imply that I haven't sinned. We all sin—we're guilty of some sins of omission as well as those we commit. But I know I could never get very far away from God. For there, in her fifth-floor walk-up apartment over the fish market on Ninth Avenue, my grandmother is praying for me daily, hourly.

It's a humble apartment—but it's rich in memories. For it's here that για-για has knelt long hours praying for her family—for me, *Dino,* her grandson. The old piano is there, that piano I played when I was just three years old. You should see it, that big old black player piano with its top that is a family picture gallery. There are pictures of the children and the grandchildren, and of the weddings and other important events in our family. No family was ever so favored, for every time her glance goes toward those pictures, my grandmother breathes a prayer for us.

You could offer her the most elegant mansion but Grandma wouldn't leave that apartment. This is the place where so many, many times God has revealed Himself to her as she has spent time in His presence.

My own heart and mind stray often to my grandmother's home, for it's there she enfolds and envelops me in her prayers. Grandma had in a very real sense prayed me into the world and she isn't ever going to abandon me to become a possible tool of Satan—not if unceasing prayer can make the difference.

I couldn't let a grandmother like her down. I couldn't let her God—and mine—down.

It's my hope and prayer that the grandmothers who read this will be encouraged, that you will realize in a new way that the grandson or granddaughter you are praying for appreciates your prayer, and is counting on you. *Please* don't let them down. Take my grandmother's contribution out of my life and there would be a great big spiritual and emotional gap in my life.

I wish you could meet my grandmother. She is really something else! I sometimes think God will have a special place for grandmothers like her, in heaven.

How can I describe her? You know, some people have an awfully distorted idea of what it's like to be a Christian. They think we're sober and joyless and kind of perpetually unsmiling. Not my για-για! The very opposite is true of her. There's something special about her. She has the most unforgettable eyes. She has a hearty laugh—and she laughs a lot. For us, as children, going to Grandma's was not like going someplace where you had to sit still, to be seen but not heard, where we had to listen to lectures on being good and so on. No. None of that. It was always a festive occasion—jolly times. We always looked forward to going to Grandma's as a highlight of our lives.

To be sure, sometimes Mom and Grandma were praying, pouring out their hearts to God. And this gave us great assurance. We knew they had this close relationship with the Lord and that we were very much a part of their prayers.

One day someone asked my sister what kind of a person Grandma is. Chris's answer was, "Grandma? She's joy personified."

At that very time, Chris was reading *The Image of Joy* (incidentally, written by my coauthor, Jeanette Lockerbie). Chris pointed to the title and said; "*That's my grandmother.* She is an image of joy, just like this book describes. She reflects Jesus—she really, truly does."

I agree with Chris. In every way, Grandma is a perfect example of what a Christian should be. She's a tremendous servant of the Lord, although she has known great sorrows and adversities (perhaps *because* of them). She'll witness like anything! She lives in New York City, and every day as she goes out shopping for her groceries and things, she'll hand out tracts. She always has a supply of Gospels of John or Mark. And when she meets some Greek people it doesn't matter who they are, she'll start witnessing to them, and she'll hand out these Gospels. Sometimes it will be a Greek priest she meets. But it doesn't matter—she doesn't care who the person is, she'll talk about Christ and try to convert him.

The thing that's so special is that Grandma is really illiterate. She can't read or write. Yet she has all this knowledge of the Lord. It's almost uncanny how she can open her Bible and point to a verse and quote it. But she can't read! (Oh, she knows a little— a very little—in English.) I can only conclude that she lives so close to the Lord, she's so sensitive and obedient to the leading of the Holy Spirit, that He more than makes up for her inability to read. I don't know how the Lord does this: I believe the Holy Spirit deals differently with different people. But I do believe He is the One who reveals things to her.

No one can dispute this, for in the end what she has foretold happens. It really does. If she told us things and then they never came to fruition, we'd all say, "Well, you know, that was just another of Grandma's tales, that the Holy Spirit had spoken to her...." But the Bible makes it clear that the proof comes when the thing *comes to pass.*

Someone has speculated that if Grandmother had lived in biblical times, she would have been one of the great women of faith such as we read about in the Old Testament. *I believe it!* I've heard some stories about her that are just incredible. She has dreams. Now, I don't believe that God speaks to people through dreams as a general thing. But I would never question or dispute my grandmother's experience. I've heard Corrie ten Boom relate that while she and her sister were in the Nazi prison, her sister had a dream that Corrie would be free and would go around the world telling her story and preaching the Gospel of Christ. It was an unlikely dream—but it came to pass! In the absence of opportunity to read His Word, God spoke to this imprisoned Christian in His own way. Why do we often try to limit God to the means we are used to? He is God and He cannot be limited.

Before the Bible was written, dreams were one way in which God communicated with people. Well, God is the same today. He will meet people's needs. And if a person who loves Him dearly cannot read His Word, He will communicate His guidance in some other way.

I'm sure I will never know, this side of heaven, just how much my grandmother prayed for me. But I do know some of the answered prayers that influenced my life tremendously. One very special instance has to do with my hitch in the army. Grandma was horrified when she heard I was in the service. She equated this with war and injury and death. (She had lost one son, so it was a reasonable equation.) In her dismay about my being in the army, she cried out to God, "Lord, get Dino out of that uniform."

Did God answer that specific prayer? You better believe it! The almost unbelievable way God engineered the whole thing—*without taking me out of the service*—well, you have to wait for another chapter to find out about that.

I don't want you to misunderstand, however, my grandmother's pure motive in asking God to get me out of that uniform. It was more than the natural concern which family members have when one of their own is in the military service of his country.

What she had in mind, this grandmother of mine, was this unshakable conviction that has never left her for one second, even before I was born, that God wanted to use me, that He had a mission for me. It might seem like presumption for a person, and particularly a simple woman like my grandmother, to come before God and appear to give the Lord orders. But it wasn't anything like that. Here is a woman who is totally committed to Christ. More than anyone I've ever met, she has the mind of Christ. She believed she was praying in the will of God. And what she was saying to the Lord was something like this:

> Lord, You and I know that You have a purpose for Dino. And You know that even before his birth, Satan was out to foil Your purpose and to destroy this boy. But you would not let that happen. And now, again, Lord, here is this attempt in another form. You know it would make the devil happy if he could have Dino killed or even injured so that his talents could not be used for Your glory. So, I'm asking, please, Father, get Dino out of that uniform.

God knows when a person is sincere, when the request really is for God's glory. And, in a wonderful way, He answered my grandmother's prayer. I don't know why God so spectacularly blesses my grandmother (except for the spiritual qualities that are so evident). But I know that He does bless her, and I get the overflow.

I wonder, sometimes, what course my life might have taken, if my grandmother had not held on to God for me at that time. And this makes me also wonder how many young people, whose parents and grandparents have dedicated them to the Lord as babies or even before, have lost out because these same parents slacked off in their prayer and example and spiritual encouragement.

Another commendable thing about my grandmother is that she never misses a church service: whenever the church door opens she is there, Sundays or weekdays. She lives alone, and we worry about her walking those New York City streets to church. She lives not too far from Glad Tidings, but even a few blocks can be too many. And they have been, for her—she has been mugged. But she can't be enticed away from the city. Once in a while she will come and stay with us in California, but her ministry is in New York City and she won't easily be persuaded to leave there. We did manage to get her to go to the Holy Land for a great conference in Jerusalem last year!

The fact that she spends so much of her time in church can readily explain why she knows so much of the Bible even though she can't read it for herself. Her faithfulness to her church, and her consistent communion with the Lord, plus her implicit obedience to the voice of the Holy Spirit put her in a prime position for sensing the mind of Christ and for praying in the will of God.

One of my grandmother's greatest charms is that she doesn't know she's any different from all the other people who profess to love the Lord. I believe she thinks everybody is as devoted to Christ as she is herself!

She reaches out to other people. They may not always understand every word she is saying, because of her mixture of Greek and English, but she's so radiant and joyful, she reflects what she feels inside. It's all over her face. Her whole being shows it. And because she is so happy, she makes other people feel happy. She even carries this brightness into her ideas of how she should dress. She loves white, and bright colors. But that's another story about my grandmother: she will not wear anything *black*.

I mentioned that she had lost a son through death. For Greek people, mourning lasts a long time. We don't easily get over losing a loved one (I'm sure this is true of people whatever their background) and black is worn for a very long time. My grandmother adhered to this strictly: black dress, black shoes and stockings— everything black. Then the Lord spoke to her in a vision and told her she was grieving the Holy Spirit by her continued mourning.

"It's not honoring to Me," the Lord indicated to her, "I am the Lord of *life*, not of death." And Grandma saw herself all robed in white. In the way that she always does, she immediately obeyed and took action on what God was telling her. From that day to this, Grandma wears only white, which she loves, or beautiful, bright colors. And she's quick to explain why, when people remark about her consistently colorful dress.

I could keep on for hours telling you about my grandmother. God bless her! Everybody should have such a grandmother!

My sister has painted a word picture of our wonderful grandmother. Let me share it with you:

> Greek in heritage
> Born unloved—but yet lovely
> Illiterate, but filled with innate wisdom
> Which makes her as the Sages of old.
>
> A life brimfull of adversities
> But emerging as conqueror over circumstances;
> A storehouse, a tower of strength
> For the weary—to come
> And replenish their spirit
>
> CHRISTINE BARTHOLOMEW

9
What Am I Doing in the Army, Lord?

Like many other Christian kids, one of the first pieces I ever played on the piano and sang was "Onward, Christian Soldiers." I was taught to love and honor my country. I'm proud to be an American!

Somehow, though, I had just never visualized myself in the army.

I had graduated from The King's College in Briarcliff, New York and they had invited me back as a teacher in the music department. I accepted, of course. It was a great opportunity to continue learning and at the same time to serve. I had my own studio there, I was given a faculty apartment, and I thought for a second that this was just the epitome! I was still very young.

It was a great experience. I had many students and I was able to work with so many talented pianists, to share my learning. At the same time it kept me up in my technique and repertoire.

I did this one year. I set up my apartment really nice and—momentarily—I was caught off guard, thinking I had "arrived."

After that first year of teaching I spent the summer in France. There, at the Fontainebleau Conservatory, outside Paris, I had the inestimable privilege of studying under such masters as Curzon, Casadesus, Rubinstein, and Boulanger. Again, to enhance my teaching ability, so that the next year I would have more to share with my students. But we didn't get through the first semester before I received a draft notice. You know—the Uncle Sam letter.

I was upset, to put it mildly. I thought: *Wow, not this!* As I've explained, it wasn't that I'm not patriotic. After all, I'd been a boy scout. I believed our country to be Number One.

But what in the world would a pianist do in the army? I couldn't imagine. "Dear Lord, why this?" I said. "There's something *wrong.*" I was questioning the Lord. Oh, I was depressed and upset. And my family also was kind of surprised by my call; they couldn't understand it either. It was an emotional time for me for two or three days. I was dejected, really. It affected everything.

Then I finally came around. I got on my knees before God and I prayed like this:

> Dear Lord, there's no choice in the matter. I've got to accept this. I've got to go into the army. You don't say yes or no to Uncle Sam. Dear Lord, I'm just leaving this in Your hands. I've always felt I was in Your perfect will, and I know this is part of Your will.

But it took me a while to come around to that point. Think of all the worry I would have been saved if I'd just accepted it at first. It wasn't really up to me to figure out *how* I would serve my country—"Theirs not to reason why. . . ."

Another thing, though, was that I didn't think I was really fit. My work hadn't prepared me for army life. That's for sure. And I just didn't understand how my ability could apply in the U.S. military.

But—I turned it over to the Lord.

We were given time—about sixty days, I think. Meantime—and again it was unmistakably God's guidance—someone had mentioned that there was an opening for a pianist in the First

What Am I Doing in the Army, Lord?

Army Band and said, "How about auditioning for it? But if you audition, you have to enlist and that's another year beyond the draft."

So I figured—Well, since I'm going to be in the service, I might as well help the Lord right along and find a place where I can be used as far as my talents are concerned.

I did audition and I passed; so I enlisted. It wasn't easy. It meant I had to give up my nice apartment, and make arrangements with the college and all that. It was a lot of adjustment.

Then, Fort Dix, New Jersey and basic training. Will I ever forget it? That was unbelievable. First thing they did was cut all my hair off. For a few minutes I felt like Samson. I thought for sure I would lose all my talent. Now that was an experience. (It was when guys were just beginning to have longer hair and to have it styled and all.)

Then came the rigid training. Mind you, it was good for me. I came out physically fit. More than I've been in my whole life. If for nothing else, army life is good for a fellow in this sense.

But while it lasted—man alive!

Still, I had a goal, and I was bound I would make it.

There's a lot of crawling in "basic"—and I crawled like mad. But my rear was always up, and I can still hear that drill sergeant bark, "Get that backside down, private!" and he would emphasize it with the toe of his boot. He was really rough.

Six weeks of it. But I had this goal that kept me going, knowing I was going to get out of this and play in the band. I made it. I came through and was assigned to the First Army Band, Fort Wadsworth, in Staten Island. It was great! I could live at home and commute each day. I was doing what I enjoyed doing in my own field—lots of rehearsals and I was the band soloist. Also, I had some students on the side, so this wasn't much change for me, really. A year and a half of this ideal situation, then. . . .

Another letter. Reassignment.

This could very easily have been Vietnam. And again—my

grandmother's prayers! It wasn't Vietnam. It was Augsburg, Germany: the Twenty-fourth Infantry Division. Oh! I thought again: Dear Lord, why did You do *this?* Why this change? The *infantry!* Do You know what that is, Lord? It's not a band. . . . I was still assigned to a band but it was a field band. (I'd found out from guys who'd been there.) What in the world was a piano player going to do out in the field? So—there it was—and again I was arguing with God.

But I had had a lot of solid training concerning God's direction in our lives and again this came to my aid. I quit fuming and said: *Dear Lord, You have a reason for this.*

I was shipped over to Augsburg, Germany, and they handed me fatigues, for the first time in my service. Before, I was wearing the dress blues: beautiful gold braid and epaulettes and all! Now here I was in army fatigues and living on the base.

I reported to the leader of the band, an officer.

"Private Kartsonakis," he said, "you will be playing the glockenspiel" (the bell lyre). This is the easiest of any instrument for a pianist to learn, because of the similarity in the way of playing.

"You'll be working with our band. You'll be on the field," he informed me.

Oh! I just cried inside of me. I just couldn't believe it. What's a concert pianist doing playing the glockenspiel: I mean, what's happening?

This went on for a week. During that week I prayed and prayed, "Dear Lord, please, I've got to get out of it. This is wrong."

Well, talk about God hearing and answering prayer! I can hardly believe it even yet. But—my grandmother's prayer. Remember what it was? Well. . . .

The very next week I received a request, right from the general's office, to come and see him. Now this—in the army—well, it was like God Himself summoning you to appear in person before Him.

I went to the general's office, more than a little nervous. I didn't know what to expect. I saluted and said, "Private Kartsonakis reporting, sir."

He replied, "Well, Dino, be seated."

Dino, he called me. Wow! I drew a deep breath and relaxed.

"I understand you are a pianist and that you play very well," he said. "I hear good reports of your work with the First Army Band, Dino. Well, my wife is giving an afternoon tea tomorrow, at the Officers' Club. Would you play some background music for this tea?"

Oh, dear Lord, is this the answer to my prayer? My mind began to race. My subconscious was saying, "Okay now: this is an opportunity—a terrific opportunity—to get out of fatigues, *if* I perform well."

"Surely, sir," I replied, "I would love to do it." Then the general talked a little about my background.

Well, next day was the afternoon tea. So I got there early, before the guests, officers' wives, began to arrive. I played a little *Dr. Zhivago,* and a little *Sound of Music,* and such: easy-listening, background music.

I found it was *more* than background music, though. The hostess came over and said, "Dino, I'm very impressed with your playing." Then she asked, "What division are you assigned to?"

I said, "It's the Artillery Division of the Twenty-fourth Infantry."

She nodded. "Okay, I just wanted to know."

And again I began to wonder: *Now, what's going to happen? I have a feeling it may be good.*

The next day I didn't have to wonder. The general sent word to my superior officer saying, "Private Kartsonakis should be reassigned to Munich, Germany, to the Officers' Club. We're impressed with his playing and we can use him in a more strategic area than in the field band."

The following day he sent two aides over and they packed for me, drove me over to Munich (about an hour or so from Augsburg) and set me up in a private room in the Officers' Club.

It was *fantastic*. I thanked the Lord from deep down in my heart. Here I was—off the base, a private room, maid service, everything.

I thought: This is great! But, Lord, do You really want me just playing in a club? Is this Your will for me right now? It's not really what I want. But if You'll help me make the most of it, I'll appreciate it.

When I arrived at the club, I had asked the officer what the general had in mind. This man explained that I would play for special functions, such as when we had high military guests coming from headquarters at Heidelberg. I was to provide the entertainment, play background music or perform concerts, and so on.

Oh, this was fantastic. It was really something else. On top of everything else, they told me if I liked, I could study in the mornings or when I wasn't working. I could go into the city of Munich and study at the Conservatory.

I almost felt guilty, things were so good. First thing in the morning when I woke up, I would stretch in my luxurious room and say, "Oh, thank You, Jesus." Then, as I looked from my second-floor window I could see beyond the beautiful grounds of this club, to where the men were out training in their fatigues. And here *I* was! It was just incredible.

"Get Dino out of that uniform," my grandmother had pleaded with God. Notice! Not "out of that *army.*" God answered her prayer to the letter. For here I was every day in Munich, wearing plain clothes, and still very much in the army.

At the same time, I did not take advantage of the situation. I was very careful. I did my job and did it well. I didn't feel I was better than the other fellows. And I continued to study—to enhance my work there. Everything went well.

It's only to be expected that there would be some who envied me, junior officers, for example, who saw where I was. Me—just a PFC. At times they were looking for something wrong in me, so they might go to the general and report, "You know that private—well, he's blowing it!"

Many opportunities to witness came my way. Some officers would come to me and say, "Dino, there's something about your music: there's a magic in it."

Even though it wasn't religious music they would sense this something. This then gave me an opportunity to tell them about my Christian background and beliefs. I wasn't obnoxious in my witnessing. I continually asked God to keep me living the Christian life. That's how I wanted to witness. And the people came to me, asking about it.

My work was very diversified. I played for our own functions on the base and gave concerts. Then I was asked to play concerts outside of the base, in auditoriums, for the Germans. This was good public relations, you see. And I would get reviews in newspapers: AMERICAN SOLDIER PERFORMS—and it would be a nice review. It was perfect. A million dollars' worth of advertising and experience. You couldn't beat it, really.

And God planned it all. He knew what I was to be doing in the army. This went on for about one year. Then my dad got sick with the beginning of his heart trouble. The Red Cross contacted me, and I was pretty upset. I talked with the general's wife and she asked if I would like to fly home and see my father. The next morning I was able to get a flight. I just wanted to see Dad, find out for myself how he was, and after a short visit with my family, I returned to Germany and completed my three-year tour of duty.

A tempting invitation then came my way. I was offered the opportunity to stay on another year and tour Europe, representing the army. It sounded good, but the Lord was speaking to me, telling me He wanted me to go back to the United States. I felt this. Nothing was verbal—it was just within me that God wanted me back in the United States.

I appreciated the wonderful offer, but I felt I had to get my discharge. I left rather sorrowfully, in a way, for everybody was so nice. I sort of hated to leave the general. But to this day we keep in touch. He watches the telecasts, and he wrote me, "I knew you were going to do well, Dino." It was a great privilege knowing him and his wife.

So I came back home to the States and the *very day I arrived*, I got a call from David Wilkerson asking me if I would like to come out to California and play for one of his youth rallies in Anaheim. The very day! This was God's seal on my returning to the States. I knew I had taken the right step.

What was I doing in the army? The Lord knew. He always does. I was just fitting into His plan, so that He could direct my life into the channels He had prepared for me—the career that began right then.

10
Keeping the Balance

"Is it hard for you to keep from becoming puffed up as success comes your way?" This is a question some people ask me, and I'm sure they ask other people whom they view as having "arrived." "Does all the applause get to you, Dino?" is another way they phrase it. And I have to admit that the temptation is there. We all have our weak points, among them the love of being praised for something we do. I constantly try to guard against this snare. I can do this only as I strive to maintain close fellowship with the Lord. Putting Him first keeps me from being knocked off balance. But it's not always easy to stay on top spiritually. It's one thing to stress this to other people. But the day-by-day attention to my own spiritual health is something else; this calls for much self-discipline. Tight schedules can be the enemy of life in the Spirit. The rushing from place to place to keep appointments, the priority that must be given to keeping in top shape professionally, can militate against the warm, intimate fellowship with Jesus Christ. But it need not.

How to handle genuine compliments is the other side of the coin. To accept the nice things people say about my performance, and to let them know it makes me happy to be able to bring pleasure and inspiration into their lives—and yet keep this balance—is not always easy. It's tough. It's *Jesus* who is to be praised. Yet, how to keep this before people without sounding pious?

What do I mean? Well, let me illustrate.

After a concert someone comes over and enthuses over how much the music meant to him. And there's no mistaking that he has been blessed. I could say a pat-sounding, "Don't thank me, thank the Lord" (which I am genuinely feeling in my heart at that moment). But this might come across to the person as a pious brush-off. How would I feel in a similar situation? I just might construe it as, "Don't come too close. I'm a performing artist, and I don't want to get involved with my audience." I know some musicians who do feel this way. They give themselves to their listeners and they feel drained at the end of the performance. All they want to do is slip away. It's not for me to judge other performers, but I don't feel this way. I really like people. It's a pleasure for me to interact with them when I've finished with my program.

And—think—what does the apparent brush-off do to the other person? It could be that when he's treated this way even once, he will develop the feeling that all Christian artists are cold and distant and unfeeling, indifferent to people as sensitive individuals. I pray God will keep me from ever being like that, or of acting in such a manner.

I believe that there is a way to keep the balance—to be properly humble and yet to give God the glory. We can graciously accept the words of commendation, then turn the spotlight upon the Lord Jesus. I can think of such instances.

Sometimes a person will say complimentary things about my playing, then add, "How do you do it?" As we chat, in a relaxed way, I'm able to point out that God gave me the talent in the first place, and that one day I'll have to give account to Him of how I have used it. (This, of course, is a Christian to whom I was talking: he would know about the biblical principle of talents.)

"I guess I don't have any talents," some say to me. And it's then I can point out that, as we read in *The Living Bible:* "God has given each of us the ability to do certain things well . . ."

Keeping the Balance

(Romans 12:6 LB)." God has given at least one talent or ability to *every* one of us. I try to encourage the person to find out what his talent is, then to pray and ask God to guide and direct as to the very best use of this God-given ability.

Some people have a variety of talents. This, too, is scriptural. I'm sure Paul must have had more than one. In fact we know of several things he did. He was a tentmaker and I can't imagine him being anything but the best kind of craftsman. We read of his oratory in Athens. (How many important things in the Bible are located in Greece!) Paul was also a healer and miracle worker for God. Yet, we hear him say, "This one thing I do" (*see* Philippians 3:13). *One thing.* But into it fed a number of things all related to Paul's supreme goal (*see* v. 14). We have to keep this in mind, to have a goal, to know what it is, and make sure that everything we do contributes toward the attaining of that goal. Maybe, if I were formulating Four Laws for The Successful Christian (which I'm not presuming to do) they would be these:

Know who God is.
Know who you are.
Know where you're going.
Know your purpose—your "one thing."

The Lord needs people in every area of life. He doesn't just work through people who are in the limelight. In fact, most of the worthwhile and lasting contributions are made by people who don't even suspect how really important they are in the Lord's scheme of things. My own grandmother is one of these people. (You're going to have to get used to meeting my wonderful grandmother in various chapters of this book. She deserves a book just about her. And she would never dream of thinking that *she* is important. But she is.)

Some Christians see other people as being special because they are in the public eye. But this is not God's criterion of greatness. He does and will continue to use those who are available, those who "report for duty" saying, "Lord, here am I," and "Lord, what will You have me to do?"

Every Christian can feel worthwhile, and that he is contributing in the world. It's always a special joy when I have the opportunity to get this truth across to young people. I pray that as they listen, then begin to put the concept into practice, life will take on great new meaning for them.

There's another facet to the matter of being able to accept honest praise. It has to do with one's self-image—how we view ourselves. The thinking of a person who has a low self-concept might go something like this: *Even if I do find out that I have some God-given talent or ability, and even if I were to work hard to perfect it, who am I that I should ever expect to be anything but mediocre? I would never make it to the top.* Such thinking, allowed to permeate the mind, all too often becomes self-fulfilling: the person doesn't get beyond the mediocre. Never able to break out of the vicious web, such people can never see themselves as being used by the Holy Spirit to influence others' lives.

Perhaps, carried to its logical conclusion, such negativism denies the power of the Lord Jesus Christ, discounts the enablement He gives to those who wholly trust Him.

We're hearing much these days about an "identity crisis." As Christians we do not need to have any identity crisis. I know who I am. This doesn't have to be a problem. I know what Jesus Christ has done in my life. I realize that the Holy Spirit is given by God to be my Teacher and my Guide through life. Knowing these things keeps me on an even keel, keeps me balanced. Ralph Waldo Emerson said, "Self-trust is the first secret of success." That's just a half-truth. We do have to trust in, believe in ourselves. But true success comes from accepting yourself, making the most of your talents, and committing your life totally to Jesus Christ. This does not diminish, rather it enhances our self-acceptance.

I believe that one of the most powerful tools that Satan wields is this distortion of a Christian's understanding of who and what we are in Christ Jesus. The Apostle Paul was undoubtedly one of the humblest men who ever lived—or God would not have so highly honored him. Yet Paul had no illusions as to who he was. By his own definition he was the chief of sinners (*see* 1 Timothy 1:15) but his former sin did not disqualify him. We don't find Paul sitting around contemplating all the factors that would classify him as unworthy. No! Paul set about to obey the Lord; he knew Christ had forgiven and cleansed him and had given him a tremendous assignment. And Paul got busy with the task.

Let me interject here that one of the genuine thrills of my life was when, just recently, I walked where the great Apostle Paul once walked. And I thought, as I was there on the Island of Crete where he had led people to Christ: *These were my people. They were Greeks.* I let my mind wander back through the centuries. What must it have been to be privileged to sit at the feet of Paul of Tarsus! To hear him proclaim the Gospel of the grace of God, the love of Christ, His life and death and glorious Resurrection —in my native tongue!

This experience made the New Testament come all the more alive for me. I was reminded that even on the day of Pentecost, there were people from Crete in Peter's audience. (For references to Crete *see:* Acts 2:11; 27:7, 12, 13, 21 and Titus 1:5.) My people heard the same message from Peter and Paul, that I heard as a child—and believed—in New York City.

All God wants in any era is for us to believe Him and hand over the reins of our life for His direction.

Like Paul, I know that "in me, in my flesh, dwelleth no good thing" (*see* Romans 7:18)—but I'm not living in the flesh. I'm living in the power of the Holy Spirit of God. That day when I asked Jesus to come into my heart, that day when I gave back to Him whatever talent He had given me, I asked Him that by His Holy Spirit He would work in me and through me.

Can I then minimize what God the Holy Spirit *is?* Can I

belittle what He is pleased to accomplish through me?

I sometimes wonder how much God-given ability is hidden under the world and the devil's "bushel"—talent that might uplift other Christians and win some lost souls to Jesus! But this talent is lost to a needy world because otherwise dedicated Christians permit themselves to be bound by a nonscriptural self-abasement, nonscriptural because it fails to take into account the indwelling Holy Spirit. Some people need to learn the balance of who they are.

Everybody wants to be "somebody"—to be special, to be known for doing one thing well. And we like to get a measure of recognition for doing it. There's nothing wrong with being good at something, striving for the top. It's not how far we go but what we do with it—what we let it do to us—that makes it "good" or "bad." Success is not immoral. To receive the plaudits of other people is not unchristian. I've met some believers in my travels who feel they can best glorify the Lord by being shy violets, and this may be very true for some of them. They may be living very close to the Lord and this is His direction for their lives. There are others, however, who hide tremendous God-given talent that could not only bless other people but which could genuinely bring glory to Jesus. Such negative feelings may have developed due to parental attitudes, or possibly the church may have fostered them with one-sided overemphasis on humility.

I have so much to thank the Lord for, in that my parents did not have these kinds of feelings about their children's abilities. My father was not yet with us, spiritually, so it was Mom who had the greater influence early in my life and my career. Hers was the attitude that God-given talent recognized as a gift from God, developed and used for Him, glorifies the Lord. This is, I believe, a balanced approach.

I know, for instance, that I could practice on the piano diligently—even twelve hours a day—but if I were to neglect to "practice the presence of Christ"—become careless as to my communion with Him—all I would have to offer would be what I, Dino, put into my performance.

I couldn't afford to let myself down like that. I can't afford to risk letting my audience down that way and I wouldn't dare let my Lord down.

People are used to hearing me announced: "And now—*Dino* at the piano!" When I step to the piano and sit down to play, I want it to be *Jesus* and Dino at the piano. That's the balance I want in my life. And to Jesus Christ be all the glory. *All* the glory.

11
It Took a Miracle

"The miracles of earth are the laws of heaven" (Jean Paul Richter).

Having read this far, are you wondering what God is going to have to do to bring my father to Himself? Perhaps you're thinking: *It's going to take some kind of a miracle!* You're right. But ours is a family in which the miraculous has been, to a great degree, God's normal dealings with us. Not that we are so special or that we have any corner on God's miracles. He delights to do the miraculous for anyone when we just *believe*.

My father was well aware of this. He lived with our praying and singing and praising the Lord. How could we have this joy in our hearts and not have some of it spill over all the time?

In Dad's case, he was never one to make it difficult for us to live our Christian life. His was a kind of passive resistance: "It's all right for you children and your mother, but I'll go my way: I'll live my own life."

What was going on in his soul those twenty years my mother and my grandmother prayed for him, the years my sister and I spent time on our knees before God for his salvation? Only the Lord knows the answer to that question.

One thing, Mom never preached and she never nagged him to go to church with us. "God can do the job," she would tell people

It Took a Miracle

who commiserated with her over her unsaved husband. "I'll pray, and try to live my Christian life before him; that's my part. God will do His." Ours was a very happy home. Sometimes I see situations where just the husband or the wife is a believer, and there's a lot of wrangling and discord. I'm so glad Mom had this insight, that harping at Dad would never have worked to bring him to the Lord. But it takes a lot of real faith just to keep sweet and trusting—and quiet.

How could we, the three of us who knew the Lord, be happy while Dad was outside the fold? How could we rejoice in the thought of the Lord's Coming—and Dad not ready to meet Him?

All I can say is that we never doubted that God would work in Dad's heart and life—that he would be saved. God would not fail to heed the prayers of a godly mother-in-law, a loving wife, and two little children. It might take a miracle—but then, we believe in miracles.

It hurt us, of course, that our daddy was not present when we saw other families enjoying themselves together. And when we would play and sing, how much greater our pleasure would have been if Dad had been there alongside Mom, to encourage and applaud us. It was a heartbreak to Mom, also, I've heard her say —for well she realized that no matter how much *she* meant to us, children need what only their father can give them emotionally.

But God was answering our prayers. Dad began to be uneasy and to have dreams and visions that disturbed his sleep lots of nights. When this happened, Mom would say, "Children, we have to pray harder for Daddy; the Holy Spirit is speaking to him." One Sunday when we came home from church Dad excitedly told Mom what had just happened:

> I was in bed—I don't know if I was asleep or awake—but my eyes were open. Suddenly something like a huge man—maybe it was the devil, I don't know—was trying to choke me to

death. I fought and struggled with the creature. Then I thought to myself: *Oh, my wife will be coming. She is a good Christian!* I prayed, "Please let her come right now," and I said to the devil or whatever it was, "My wife is coming; she is a good Christian. She believes in Jesus." The thing left that very minute.

"And," Dad told Mother, "just as it disappeared down the steps, you came to the door." From time to time there were other signs that God was not letting our dad be happy in his unsaved condition. So we kept on praying.

How did the great change come in my father's life?

It wasn't in church. There was no preacher present. He wasn't reading his Bible or listening to a Christian program on the radio —none of these things (good as each of them is). He was alone with his thoughts and his Maker. But let Dad tell you himself. (If you listen you'll hear his Greek accent.)

> All those years my wife and my children had been praying for God to save me. Well, one day I was thinking about my life: *I work and work and work. I go out with my worldly friends and I drink and I smoke and I play cards. But what will be the end of it all? I know how to do better, for I have a fine Christian wife and a Christian son and a Christian daughter.*
>
> I knew I was getting along in years. So, that very day I asked God to show me something to make me understand, to open my mind, and make this my last day to resist the Holy Spirit. I got down on my knees and said, "O Jesus, answer my prayer; let me know You are powerful. I will give up everything of the world: all the smoking and drinking and card playing and everything else that does not please You. Only save me— forgive me for all my sins and for not believing on You all these years—and I will never go back anymore."

Jesus heard my prayer. A light started to come in and I felt a kind of power going all through my body. I felt clean all over, as clean as I feel today. Now, in the power of the Holy Spirit, I can enjoy all the good things my wife and children enjoy in Jesus.

Yes, it took a miracle. But isn't it the greatest of miracles each time someone passes from death unto life. Isn't the New Birth always a miracle?

I know it hurts my father sometimes as he thinks of those years we could all have been rejoicing together and enjoying the things of the Lord. But the important thing is that God did not let him go—He continued to speak to him and the Holy Spirit never gave up. And now we are truly *one in the Spirit and one in the Lord*.

Dad tells a story about me and the movies. When I was quite young, he and I would walk down to Times Square and look around the stores and watch the interesting people that were always milling around there. One day Dad said, "Let's go into a movie, Dino. I would like to see this movie."

I didn't want to go. Dad remembers that I said to him, "What if Jesus should come! I wouldn't want to be in a movie house when He comes."

So Dad agreed that I could walk on home and he would go alone to the movie. But I didn't go home. Two hours later, when he came out, there I was waiting for him. This touched him and he apparently never forgot it.

My father has had a great deal of sickness in his life and it's just wonderful how the Lord has preserved his life through some severe surgeries.

Just a little over a year ago his doctor gave Dad the verdict that he had only two months to live due to a critical heart condition. The surgeon recommended open-heart surgery, but could not give a good prognosis due to all the other medical problems that could complicate Dad's case.

"Talk it over with your family," the surgeon said. "Either way, it's a chance you're taking. But without the heart surgery, there's no possible way you can live longer than about two months."

We talked it over and we prayed earnestly for the Lord's will. Then Dad came up with his own announcement: "I'll trust the Lord, and go through with the surgery."

So this is what happened. First, my father talked with the surgeon who was going to perform the heart surgery. "Doctor," he asked, "do you believe that God is going to use your hands as you perform this operation?"

The surgeon looked at him and answered, "Without God I can't do anything."

For a few days after the surgery Dad didn't know any of us. He was in the Intensive Care unit and we came and went without his recognizing any of us. Then one day he opened his eyes and there he saw me—and with me, Miss Kathryn Kuhlman. He recognized us. We had come to pray with Dad. How we all rejoiced at the goodness of the Lord in bringing my father through this severe operation.

Dad had come a long way since he committed his life to Christ: he now believed in miracles, for they are a normal part of our Christian experience!

Another thing I remember about my father is his wisdom in certain situations. Growing up in New York City had its hazards: in my high-school days drugs were already a menace. It was hard to escape, living as we did in the Bronx at that time. I remember what it was like to have dope forced on me. "Buy it . . . or else" —and the alternative didn't look inviting. Those were the days of brass knuckles and switchblades, and you never knew what the day would bring.

One day, near the end of the school year, I arrived home pretty upset. I never felt any temptation to experiment with the stuff but it had been as much as my life was worth that day not to give

It Took a Miracle

whatever money I had to the student pusher. I had thrown the dope away, and I told my father the whole story. I still remember how he talked to me.

"Dino," he said, "you don't have to *smoke* that marijuana. But you don't need to get yourself killed, either. Give them the fifty cents or whatever it is this gang demands. It's just for a few more days and school will be out."

You'll note it was my Dad I told, not my mother. If I'd mentioned this to her, she would have gotten all excited and she would have torn up to that high school so fast—and probably created a scene. Nobody would have gotten away with pushing her kid around. But Dad's way was the wiser in this instance. I've always appreciated this.

My father owned a restaurant and as we grew older, Chris and I helped out there. And there, too, you never quite knew what might happen. This was New York City!

For instance, one day I was working at the cash register when —Whammo! A man dashed in, ran over to where a customer was eating his meal at the counter, and stabbed the man. The weapon used was a big tailor's scissors. It was a sickening sight. The attacker was obviously in a frenzy and we were afraid of what he might do next. Dad tells that I gave one leap right over the counter and out the door. Meanwhile, he made for the kitchen to grab up a pan of hot grease to throw at the attacker. However, help came and he didn't have to do this.

Life in New York City is filled with many memories. None is more precious than the way God answered our prayers and saved my father. Even if it did take a miracle!

12
Taking and Making Opportunities

"No opportunity is ever lost—someone else picks up the ones you miss" (author unknown).

I read somewhere that the doors of opportunity are marked PUSH. Whether this is true or not, I don't know. I do know, though, that when God gives us a talent to use for Him we have to seize the opportunities available to us.

With God-given ability there is a corresponding responsibility. We must not hoard the talent. We must not bury it. God wants you and me to be good stewards of what He has entrusted to us. So when He unlocks doors of opportunity it's up to us to step in, not sit around waiting for God to do it all.

God will get His work done. If one person will not make godly use of his talent, I believe that the Lord will give the talent to someone who *will* honor Him through it.

One of the important aspects of taking opportunities is that you believe in yourself. Recognize that you do have talent and that when you've committed it to Christ, He will help you to be what He wants you to be.

Opportunities come in all sizes: small, medium, and large. If we really are asking the Lord to guide us, we need to be willing to serve Him in the lowly as well as in the big important places. There's a biblical principle here: "He that is faithful in that which is least, is faithful also in much . . ." Jesus said (Luke 16:10).

It always interests me that in every area of life scriptural principles apply. God does not violate them in everyday life. The Lord is very practical. And He knows we need the smaller successes if we're going to be able to handle the bigger ones later on. A quick rise to fame can create problems in a person's own life and in our attitudes toward other people.

Somehow it's easier when we come up the hard way. Although, don't let me give you the idea that anything was all that hard for me (at least I didn't recognize it). Give me a piano—and I am at home. That is my territory. I've heard it said that every artist has a "true country" and the piano is mine. So it's been just great!

I believe that no matter what field we are in, when we're doing the thing God has equipped us to do well, we're happy in doing it. I sometimes wonder how many people go through most of their lives just dragging themselves to a job. It's not something they delight in, something they would do just for the joy and fulfillment it gives them, something they would even do for *nothing*.

Sometimes I would like to say to young people, "Wouldn't it be a good idea to sit down and consider, 'I'm likely to be working most of my life at something. What would I most like to do?' " We usually like to do the thing we're good at naturally, something we can have success in doing. Psychologists tell us that for emotional stability and a good self-image every one needs to have some success experiences. I believe this.

So, early in the game, it's wise to find out what you *enjoy* doing. I was three years old when I found what I liked to do. That's pretty young! But I've never changed my mind.

But if we're going to both take and make opportunities, we have to train in the areas of our ability. It usually means self-discipline and hard work. I can't see how God would use a lazy Christian or how a slothful person can glorify Him.

The Lord has been extra generous to me in the way He has showered opportunities on me. I can never be sufficiently grateful to Him. Not only has He given me a talent to use for Him—He also gave me the sense to know that talent in itself is not enough. As I shared with you earlier in this book, it's my belief that it was the Holy Spirit who instilled in me the resolve to excel—to be satisfied with giving God nothing short of my best.

Another thing: God provided the opportunities for me *in the direction of His will for my life.* This is extremely important. Sometimes I wonder, seriously, where I would be and what I would be doing if my mother had not been adamant that my talent *be used for God.* I was never permitted to forget it (even if I had wanted to). Mom has even said, "Dino, God gave you that great gift, and I believe that if you ever used it in ways that would not honor Him, He might take it away from you." This isn't the time or place to go into a theological discussion of how God deals with us in such situations. But I know that the only really happy way to live is to yield to Christ, let the Holy Spirit have His way in your life, and serve the Lord with everything you have.

I've known young people who have godly parents. These young people have many gifts but they've turned them to their own advantage and for worldly gain. And they have totally lost out. Money is not a source of happiness. Happiness is being in the will of God. (Now there's a good HAPPINESS IS . . . slogan!)

My opportunities to serve the Lord came while I was very young. Playing for Children's Church on Friday after school, and in the various Sunday services and a number of other ministries in and around New York City. All of these gave me the chance to exercise my talent. And, undoubtedly, this was a motivating factor. In addition to playing the piano for the sheer love of it, and practicing my lessons to please my teacher, there was always an outlet for my talent, an exciting real-life thing going on. I needed to keep on learning—I still do. One never arrives. But the opportunities were there. I was, as we say, where the action was, and this spurred me on.

Taking and Making Opportunities

If it had been (1) that the opportunities were not there or (2) that I had not grasped them, it's doubtful that the Lord would have blessed and advanced me to the place of service He has given me today. This, to me, is the essence of the stewardship of God-given talents.

It's encouraging to remind ourselves that God will hold us accountable only for the ability He has given us. God is just. He is fair. But He *does* expect returns. The parable of the Talents makes it abundantly clear that this is so.

I have some young people say to me, "But Dino, I have just one talent."

I would like to say to you if you're thinking along that line, "You'd better invest that one talent for Jesus; get some interest on it for Him." And when we do this—invest what God has committed to our trust—it won't matter to Him if it's one little talent or ten big ones. You and I will have the joy of hearing Jesus say, "Well done, good and faithful servant" (*see* Matthew 25:23).

Why was the unprofitable servant in the Gospels rebuked? For *not taking the opportunity* afforded him by his one talent.

Some people are waiting till they are "good enough." Meanwhile, needs go unmet, needs which they could fill with their present capability and make a worthwhile contribution. It's debatable in my mind whether a person will be really used by the Lord if he is not willing to say, "Lord, You know where I'm at right now. You know there are others who can do this thing better than I can. But Lord, I'm here and the need is here and there doesn't seem to be anybody else . . . so if You'll help me, I'll pitch in and do my best."

I believe God is looking for people with this kind of spirit, who will both take and make opportunities to serve Him. What do I mean by "making opportunities"? In a word—volunteer! We sing "A Volunteer for Jesus" and this sounds good. But we need to activate what we're singing about. Jesus needs volunteers. As you read earlier, my sister and I were not hesitant in volunteering our services, as Chris puts it. We loved to sing, so we sang. We made our own opportunities. One led to another.

There is no such thing as instant success. *If it were that easy everybody would be doing it.* Young people and older ones, too, tell me they have ability. They're talented, but they're discouraged because they don't get the opportunities they see me getting on stage and on television. They want this instant success and I tell them there is a lot more to it than the eye can see. There's plenty of hard work. There are demands, and responsibilities. Through constantly being exposed, I grew into all of it. There were the opportunities we've described before: in church and Sunday school and youth groups and so on. It's this thing of being available when there is a job to do. Generally what looks like instant success is really something earned the hard way. The exceptions these days are some of the rock groups that appear to be an instant success. But how long does it last? Not very long. Some fall flat on their faces. And, oh—the letdown. Sometimes the result is that their lives are destroyed entirely.

But when you have the ability that God has given you, it's all so different. God is very practical and there's a great concept here. He could make me or anybody else an instant success—overnight. He could easily put me where the whole world would hear me, with no effort on my part. But God knows us. He knows how very human we are, how fallible, how fickle. So I'm glad for the way the Lord has led in my life and that I can see His direction all the way.

Back to what I mentioned about believing in yourself. This is so important, for distrust of oneself keeps many a Christian from the real blessing of serving Christ. Pastors tell me of the problems they have in filling niches. For instance, a woman was approached about playing the piano for a department in Sunday school. People who had heard her play at home recommended her to the director of Christian Education who was frantically trying to fill various positions, with limited talent in the church.

Taking and Making Opportunities

"I'm not good enough," this woman said. Good enough for what—for whom? For herself, so that people would compliment her? This happens. I know it does. So she missed her opportunity. And I know that one opportunity leads to another when we give the best we have to God. There are others like this woman. They would rather sit on the sidelines where it's safe—where they won't risk hitting a wrong note—than venture their talent and help out. Maybe they've never heard what a friend of mine once told me: "God can only direct a moving object."

So you're *not* a Rubenstein! You know you have *some* talent, and God knows you have it, for He gave it to you. The thing to do, then, is offer it back to Him, dedicate yourself and your talent to Jesus.

After dedication comes discipline—the hard grind to sharpen this tool that God has given you to work for Him. I learned very early that God had given me a very special talent. But I had to do the practicing. The Holy Spirit doesn't do this for you. What He does, though, is to give you a confidence, a poise when you really do your part. He helps you to feel inside, "I can do it. I *can*, for God, for His glory."

Here, to summarize what I've been saying about opportunities, are these few steps:

> Recognize that you do have a God-given talent. Remember, everybody does!
> Dedicate the talent *and yourself* to the Lord.
> Discipline yourself to train to be the best in your field, *for God.*
> Believe you can do it.

Take every opportunity no matter how seemingly small. It might be the very door God is unlocking for some future big work for Him.

As we *walk with the Lord in the light of His Word* and try to be our very best for Him, it's exciting! We never know what God has in store for us. I just can't wait to see what He's going to do next!

Talent? Yes, it's important. But it's just one piece of the picture. We have to be on the alert to take and make opportunities to use this talent to glorify Jesus Christ.

Then—be ready for life with a capital *L*.

13
What More Can a Secretary Ask?

This is one part of the book that came as a complete surprise to me until it was almost time for it to go to the publisher. To be sure, I had heard my secretary and Jeanette Lockerbie kidding around one day when the three of us were in my office in Hollywood.

"Maybe I should interview *you*," Jeanette had quipped. "That should be a sure way to find out a thing or two. What kind of a boss is Dino, anyway?"

I didn't know, though, that they had actually gone through with it and that this chapter had been contributed, until it was handed to me. I assure you it was totally unsolicited on my part.

I've certainly been fortunate in having such a wonderful person for my first secretary. She loves the Lord and is sensitive to the leading of the Holy Spirit. These are prime qualities, in my estimation.

What does a secretary look for in a new boss—good looks, a cheery *good morning* as he presents a rose he picked from his neighbor's favorite rose bush or one who says, "Thank you," every time you lift a finger for him? None of these really mattered when I was asked to be Dino's secretary. His brother-in-law had interviewed me, since Dino was out of the city. I had heard that artists and such gifted people usually were very difficult to work for as they were temperamental, high-strung perfectionists. I had only seen Dino at Kathryn Kuhlman's miracle services in Los Angeles (on three occasions) and on her telecast *I Believe in Miracles* many times. But I had never heard him speak and knew absolutely nothing about him. But I knew God had asked me to work for Him and that was good enough for me.

With no previous introduction or knowledge of a new employer, there is always that anxious moment of meeting and "breaking the ice." He knew nothing about me and probably wondered what they had chosen for him as a secretary. In fact, he is probably still wondering, months later. Actually I was doing his work for several days before we met. Then the morning came when, without any forewarning, this handsome, well-trimmed, smartly dressed, smiling gentleman joyfully came bounding into the office with: "Hi! I'm Dino." As if I didn't know. But he seemed more handsome than I had remembered from television or the second balcony at the Shrine Auditorium, and so warm and friendly. No wonder he always says, "Make the letters warm." It comes naturally for him because he is just that: warm. I liked his enthusiasm, his sincerity, and what a great sense of humor! I realized then he had more than one gift—they were multiple and how could I have been so fortunate to work for him!

My opinion has not changed or wavered for a moment. This is still my impression and opinion of one of the finest, most talented, and brilliant young men in America. Without any reservation, we who work for and with him feel he is an all-American young man to be proud of, and a great ambassador for Christ as well as our country.

What is it like to work with a man like this? Wonderful—and he really works with you. I could expect a call in the morning about 7:15 with a: "Hi! It's Dino!" I'd say: "Dino at the piano?" and he'd reply, "No, Dino who just shaved. How's everything going?" Before he would start sharing business there was always that sincere personal touch. He had already been working and practicing but never failed to "check in," keep me informed of his whereabouts, constantly checked and rechecked his itinerary and every facet that went into the making of a good concert: special music for orchestration, tape background, mikes, and so on. He was always on top of everything and totally involved in his musical ministry.

He is very attentive to things at the office and insists on reading all his mail when he returns from concerts and, if possible, insists that all correspondence and album orders receive a response within twenty-four hours and he doesn't just demand it—he helps it to happen.

For instance, I remember once we were inundated with requests for records. We were in a record promotion and the orders were coming in by the hundreds each day. We had set up an assembly line with his grandmother, who was visiting in California, as straw boss, his mother and aunt working there day after day. On this particular day Dino was in the lineup, too, wrapping, sealing, addressing, and posting records. Hours into the day, with sweat running down both cheeks, he looked up at me smiling, with that twinkle in his eyes, and said, "People say they envy me. I wonder if they would envy me now!" He looked down at his two dirty, sticky hands, laughed heartily, and picked up another stack of records.

It was the norm, not only after a concert road trip but during it, for Dino to call and say, "I want you to write a couple of letters for me and send each person a record. The first one is to a lovely lady I met on the plane and I promised her that I would be praying for her. She is ill. Make it very warm and tell her we'll be praying for her—and please send her a record." Or "There is a young lady I met on the street in such and such a city. She recognized me and said her dad was a fan of mine. Here is his address. Write a note saying I met his daughter and how proud he must be to have such a lovely young lady for a daughter . . . send a record." Or "Mr. and Mrs. So-and-So were so kind to me. Write and thank them." With each he would give a "for instance" of things they had done or said. When he returned from this particular trip it was just a continuation of the same—a list of names and business cards. It was very easy for me to make them warm as you can see, for he really is a very warm person.

He's generous to a fault and very thoughtful of his family, friends, and business associates. I treasure little notes he would tuck in with gifts for special occasions, from trips, or an I-appreciate-you gift. Flowers were his specialty and my very first long-stemmed roses came from Dino.

I remember on one occasion when I was moving from one apartment to another, he asked with concern how I was coming and if I had adequate help. I assured him I did. He walked over to my desk, plunked down a crisp, new bill and said: "I want to help, too." I could take up a chapter just on "for instances" like this.

But no one is perfect—what are his weak points and faults? Well, he gets nervous! Very nervous! Especially just before a big concert (as playing with a symphony) and he wears out the carpet in the office, especially around my desk as he paces back and forth with the phone in his hand. He will keep asking, "Do you think I can do it?" He underestimates himself and seems to need constant reassuring. Perhaps a perfectionist is never sure until it's over, but I would always insist he had done it before and left them clapping in a stand-up position. "They wouldn't have asked you if they didn't think you could do it," I would assure him. "Of course you can do it. You're great!" And he is.

Another weak point: vulnerability to people who would exploit or take advantage of him and his talent. Some of his biggest disappointments and disillusionments have probably come this way. But he would always reply without malice that no matter

What More Can a Secretary Ask? 113

what others did he must be Christlike and do the right thing. And he always did.

He has difficulty in saying no. Consequently he sometimes finds himself with commitments beyond what one human should have. So we have to juggle appointments, dates, times. We do get into some sticky situations but this is never because Dino is not organized, or that he doesn't care. Rather, it's because he just tries to do too much for too many and his work is enough to keep three people busy, apart from taking on extra assignments.

His thoughtful ways and lack of *no* in his vocabulary have inadvertently encouraged many a young lady. His smiles have been taken seriously as *personal*—and then would come the letters! There are usually several one-sided romances going on, with each girl "knowing" that God meant Dino for her. We have the delicate task of saying, "Thank you" (for *"No,* thank you")—without hurting the young lady. We try to let her know that it's just Dino's friendly way; that he shares his Christian love and his enthusiasm with all, but that for the present his work and his career demand all his attention and time.

He is still young enough to think serious thoughts after he has climbed the rungs. For now it is all business, with very little time for anything else apart from his own family, to whom he is very devoted and attentive. It's just beautiful to see him with his grandmother. I recall one occasion when Dino took her shopping for clothes in Beverly Hills. And they didn't go alone—Miss Kuhlman who has the highest regard for Dino's grandmother, Mrs. Frudakis, accompanied them on the shopping spree. And from the reports they brought back, they must have had fun! Grandmother knew exactly what she wanted: a dress in the same style she had bought fifty years before. (At that, she was probably quite up-to-date, come to think of it!) The same with a hat. She wanted the style she was used to. And if it was to be had, you can be sure that Dino saw to it that his beloved grandmother got what she wanted.

Being Dino's secretary is fascinating. Never a dull moment! Do I like my job?
What "job"?

It's a *pleasure* to be part of such a great ministry for the Lord and none of it is really work.

14
On the Go With God

"Your son will be heard all over the world."

I was quite young when the Lord revealed to my mother that her son would have a wide, even a world ministry. At the time this may have seemed unlikely to other people but not to my mom. She's a great *believer*.

In the providence of God—with His directing hand on my life—I have been privileged beyond my own expectations. Through travel and by means of television, I really have been heard in many countries. And I'm by no means through. In fact, I think I'm just at the beginning of the tremendous things God has in store for me as long as I put Him first in my life.

What's it like, this on-the-go life?

I know some people envy me. They say, "I wish I could go to all the places you go and meet the people you meet." They see my life as totally glamorous. It doesn't, seemingly, occur to them that there are two sides to the travel coin. Not that I'm complaining. No! I appreciate so much all the good things the Lord brings into my life—much of it connected with my traveling ministry. I love the life He has given me. But I am also realistic.

There's a powerful missionary hymn that goes like this: "I'll go where You want me to go, dear Lord; I'll be what You want me to be."

In the fervor of spiritual emotion such as when we are in a great service and the Holy Spirit is moving on hearts, many people go forward and they say to God, "I'll go where You want me to go." And I believe that most of them sincerely mean it at the time. God knows our hearts; we dare not judge other people or their actions or speculate as to their motives.

But, without a doubt, it's one thing to make a vow before God: it's another to keep it. If you don't mean it, forget it!

Personally, I wouldn't change one day of my walk with God. I would, however, caution other people even as I remind myself, "Be careful about the promises you make to God that you will go, *and keep on going,* where He wants you to go, unless you are prepared to accept all that this may involve."

There's the travel itself: often the hassle and frustration of delays and of lost luggage, of travel documents, and of not always knowing the language. And it's a good thing, as my mother often tells people, that I started on a rickety old piano, for I've played all kinds since. Mom and Dad laugh over how I would have to lift up the keys while playing in some churches where a number of the piano keys stuck.

Being what the Lord wants me to be is often harder than going where He wants me to go. It's only the time spent alone with Him that gives me the right spirit, that keeps me sweet when things don't always work out right.

Another of the costs of being in a traveling ministry is the emotional price one pays in being away from friends and family much of the time. The concert is over. The applause has died down. There's the last handshake, the final "God bless you for your ministry" and while the audience goes on home, the visiting artist usually makes his way to an impersonal, however comfortable, hotel or motel.

Again, let me say that I'm serving the Lord by choice. I love what I'm doing. But I'm presenting the human side, the part that many young people do not consider when they take their step of dedication to the Lord.

What makes it all worthwhile? I'll tell you. We never say, "I'll go, dear Lord," without having His sweet assurance, "I'll go with you." Jesus said, "Lo, I am with you always" (*see* Matthew 28:20). *Always.* When everything is going just fine, and also when, as will happen some days, everything goes wrong, or seems to. The bright days and the dark days. The times when we feel, "I can do it." And the days when we are not all that sure. All the days, Jesus is there. He really is!

I've learned, too, that God is reasonable. He doesn't make unrealistic demands of anyone. When the schedule is too full, it's not always all God's leading. So it takes prayer and much waiting on God. It's not His will that we should rush-rush-rush from one engagement to another with never time to refresh our souls. No one can be at his best for God if he is functioning on his own steam. This is why I see to it that I schedule time to come home, to practice, to be alone, to pray: to become fresh. I could never make it and be at my best for God, apart from these times of refreshment.

Another thing to guard against is this: So often, in a work for God, we involve other people and they begin to call the shots. Then, before you know it, they are controlling your ministry. You have to remember that God calls you to a particular job. The person who is called often finds himself being controlled by other people. And there's not the sensitivity to the direct leading of the Holy Spirit. This is all-important.

I've had the experience of keeping up a grueling schedule yet sailing through it without any feeling of being frazzled. That's when I've felt so strongly that it was God's leading for me to keep going. We need to keep the channel open between the Lord and ourselves. We need to be sensitive to His voice. This is the secret of daily guidance.

Many times I'm asked, "Dino, what is the most exciting assignment the Lord has ever given you?"

That takes some thinking over. It depends on how the person defines *excitement*. The most exciting? This just *had* to be the time when I was only seven years old and I was asked to play for the main church service on Sunday at Glad Tidings. This was a new experience, and it was something I had dreamed of when I was even younger. I had never doubted that it would come to pass. And now here I was—just seven and invited to do it. I remember that I was unbelievably thrilled when I found myself actually doing this. That was my first and still most memorable engagement.

Actually, excitement is a part of belonging to the Lord and being used in His service. You cannot be in partnership with Him and not be thrilled. If ever I were to wake up in the morning without this feeling of excitement I've known all my life, I would certainly want to check my spiritual barometer to see if it's still working. Excitement is not something *I* maintain; it's something that courses in my veins when I think of all that Jesus has done and is going to do through me.

Take the television ministry, for instance. The thrill of reaching millions of people when I'm not even at the keyboard. This is one of the best ministries anyone could ever have. Investing your life. It's almost like the business world. And what dividends in sheer fulfillment! Sometimes it happens that I'm playing a concert at the same time a telecast is on. (My parents never dreamed they would have more than one Dino!)

The *variety* of opportunities certainly adds excitement. Among the interesting assignments recently was the Prayer Breakfast in Washington, D.C., sponsored by the National Religious Broadcasters. This is an annual function to which some of the nation's top leaders of government come. It was a privilege to perform at this Prayer Breakfast, and an inspiration to know that God has His people in high places. This should encourage us and challenge us to pray for these men and women in our critical times.

On the Go With God

The annual convention of the Christian Booksellers Association was another eye-opener for me. I had the pleasure of playing for this gathering of some four thousand conventioneers. It was just great meeting so many of the very people who handle my albums and who may be selling this book. I never dreamed that Christian book selling was on such a grand scale! It's no wonder, though, with such enthusiastic people dedicated to this ministry.

There's another part of the traveling that I want particularly to mention. That is, all the people who help to make the performance possible: the pastors, the music directors, the ushers, the people who work on publicity—a whole host of background persons (except that on God's crew there is *never* background personnel. God has no *little* jobs). It takes so many, since there are numerous details, big and small. And somebody has to stick with each one or else there will be confusion.

I can always sense when the preparations have been adequate. There's a relaxed atmosphere. And I'm sure the Holy Spirit has more freedom to work than when things are last minute and hectic. God is not the Author of confusion, the Bible tells us. So we can be certain that it is His will that we do things in an orderly manner.

How can I thank each of you who has contributed so much to the smoothness—yes, the success—of a performance? I really wish I could meet you personally, every one of you, and shake your hands and get to know you. How about when we all get to heaven? Maybe we'll have time up there. In the meantime, please accept my warm and heartfelt thanks. I know that God has already blessed you for what you've done in His Name. It is said that doing a thing well is it's own reward. This is true. But I want you to have a great big measure of joy, besides.

And the *audience?* What would any performance be without

the listeners? You have been so good, so responsive, so appreciative, so generous in your comments. I just want you to know that I appreciate you, and you—and especially YOU!

Sometimes things do go askew. Not long ago, for example, people were lined up waiting to get into an auditorium where I was performing. It was a very hot evening and folks were becoming disgruntled. They wanted to get inside where it was air-conditioned.

What was the holdup?

Are you ready for this one? The Steinway, specially ordered for this concert, *was just being delivered!*

I don't know quite what the problem had been with the delivery. But you know, as I recall that particular concert, I can still feel the sweet spirit of that audience. You could sense the presence of the Holy Spirit. I had great freedom as I spoke between the numbers. There was such joy! It was contagious. I couldn't see the faces for the spotlight—but I could feel that people were smiling. They were happy.

It must have been that the people who planned that concert (a group of churches) had really prayed that the Lord would bless. And He did—even if the piano *was* late!

That's not the worst thing that ever happened to me while on the go. . . . I'm thinking of an evening in San Francisco. Between numbers, as I often do in my concerts, I reach for the microphone and talk a little about the Lord. I did so that night. And wow! The mike was live—I don't know how many volts. I went down like a tree felled by lightning. I was really out. I must have been carried from the stage though I was unaware of anything. People didn't know what had happened but they knew that whatever it was, it wasn't good. I remember, as I came to, the first word on my lips was *Jesus.* I repeated His Name. Then, to the amazement of the men standing over me, I began to rise to my feet. "I have to get back in there," I insisted. I walked back onstage and played as though nothing had ever happened.

Later, I learned how very serious the situation had been. A major electrical problem had developed, shooting an overload of power into the microphone, enough to have welded my hand to the metal stand. *But God didn't let that happen!*

I never cease to thank Him for the miracles that are all around us if we only believe and recognize His hand on our lives. He is the *God of miracles.* I believe this.

Would you like to hear about the concert I almost missed?

The Lord has been so good to me and I've never missed one engagement, never been too sick or too late or too anything. God has been with me and I've always made it. I praise Him for this.

Well, not long ago, I stepped onto the rostrum of a large church—Lakewood Baptist, in the Long Beach area of California—and as I sat down at the piano I thought: *Well, Dino, this is one concert you almost missed!* And I could almost visualize myself in a Greek Army uniform. (I'd seen them and they're not very good-looking.)

Just days before, I had been in Athens when the Cypress-Turkey situation exploded. All flights to the United States were being cancelled. There I was, the right age and of Greek parentage. Not only this, but my parents were also there visiting at the time. The whole setup. I could see myself—all the hair off again! But that was not God's will for me this time and I was able to get on the very last flight leaving for the U.S.A. My parents had to wait two weeks for a flight.

I don't take such things for granted. I believe that this, too, was one of God's miracles with which He surrounds us.

It's so good to know that no matter where we are, whether the Lord calls us to a hometown ministry or to something that keeps us on the go, *He is there.* I really feel that He is—I feel His presence with me.

I believe that what really, truly counts most is knowing I am in God's will. This makes for contentment in whatever state we find ourselves, as the Apostle Paul puts it (*see* Philippians 4:11).

Yes, I'm on the go. But—on the go *with God.*

15
It <u>Can</u> Happen to You

Everybody has some heroes. We look at another person and we say, "If only I could be what he is"; or "If I had the same kind of job"; or "If God had given me this or that talent." Somehow it's hard for people to be satisfied with who they are and what they are doing.

Not that there's anything wrong with looking up to people. For me there is the great Artur Rubinstein. Now there is a *pianist!* I admire this man for many things besides his superb playing. He's so honest. He doesn't seem to have any hang-ups like so many leading artists. He's the greatest! And yes—I could very easily find myself wishing that I could be what he is.

I can understand, then, when someone comes up after a service and says, "Dino, you seem to have it made. Yours is the model life. You're so fortunate to know where you are and where you're going." Then, usually with a world of longing in their eyes, they add, "If it could only happen to *me!* How can I have a life like yours?—secure in the ability you have. You seem like you just can't miss."

Maybe it's just a case of the grass on the other side of the fence appearing to be greener. Or it could be that the person really has a strong desire to have God use him. I have no way of knowing. But, since people do share this longing with me, I take the opportunity to try to encourage them.

I tell them that this is for everyone. God does not play favorites. His Word tells us that He is no respecter of persons. And I make it very plain that I'm far from ideal, or a model, as they say. I know myself better than anyone. I know my own weaknesses. And let me say right here, that to me, the biggest sin a person can commit *as a Christian* is to be aware of sins and shortcomings and failings in our own lives—and not do something about it!

One of the special ministries of the Holy Spirit in our lives is to convict us of sin—particular sins. Then, the Bible tells us, "If we confess our sins, he is faithful and just to forgive us our sins, and to cleanse us from all unrighteousness" (1 John 1:9).

I try to impress on young people and others who share with me their own longings, that the place to begin is *to commit their life to Christ.* That is Number One, if we want God to use us.

Then, God's Word is vital in the growth of a believer. I can never overemphasize this. All Scripture is given by inspiration of God. Every word of it! It has also given me the richness and direction for my life as I read and study and meditate on God's Word! It's astounding to some people that the answer to certain questions and problems and the provision for needs is right there, written in the Word of God. So, if we want to be the kind of person God can bless and use, it's all-important that *we read the Bible*—the Christian's Manual.

Third, *"Pray without ceasing"* (1 Thessalonians 5:17). This is the relationship with Christ that is always there. It's getting up in the morning and first thing saying, "Thank You, Jesus. Thank You, Lord." Instant communication with Jesus Christ. We don't have to do prayer setting-up exercises. We don't have to have an appointment and wait till the hour strikes. And, because of the daily, hourly praying without ceasing, when some trouble comes, or some problem arises, you then automatically signal to heaven. Jesus is *there,* interceding for us, representing us. But oh, we forget—we forget that Jesus Christ is there to meet our needs whatever they may be.

It _Can_ Happen to You

I realize that even as I'm encouraging you who ask, "How can this happen to me?" I'm speaking to myself. I'm urging my own heart to have a perfect trust, to *really* count on the presence of Jesus. I, too, need answers. And so often I try to work things out by myself, forgetting that Jesus is there to meet this very need that I have—as small, as simple as it may be—or as great.

There's a song I put on my latest album. Ralph Carmichael wrote it. It's titled "My Little World," speaking of how we all create our own little world. And I don't know if it is self-pity or false modesty or what have you—but we seem to think that our sphere is so little, so insignificant—that our need is too small for Christ to care about and meet. We forget that He sees us in our little world. I'm thinking of those miracle services. Many times there are those who see others being healed and they think: *Their condition is more serious than mine* or: *They are more important than I am and I should just forget about my need.* But it's not true! This is not the way to think. God wants to answer even that small prayer—meet that seemingly insignificant need. That's how great God is!

So, as I tell other people—and myself at the same time—it's important, if we would be in God's perfect will, that we read His Word and maintain a close relationship with Jesus Christ through constant prayer and meditation. Jesus makes this so plain, so simple, when He tells us that men ought always to pray, and not to faint (*see* Luke 18:1). We have this tremendous option:

Pray and keep strong.
Fail to pray—and grow weak and faint and faltering.

It's up to us, you and me—what we do about this.

King David knew this open secret of keeping in the perfect will of God. And remember, David was a great musician as well as the beloved king of Israel! He meditated day and night: he kept the warm glow of faith alight in his life.

What happens when we live this close to the Lord? It's amazing the sensitivity this gives one. You can tell in an instant if you're making the wrong move. It's as though a literal voice said, "Turn around; this is the way; walk ye in it." And, of course, this is the Holy Spirit.

In my playing, I need this sensitivity. When I step out on the stage, I have to feel that the Holy Spirit is directing me all the way. I never play a piece the same way twice. I couldn't do that, for each audience is different; they have different needs. And I want to feel their needs; I want the Holy Spirit to keep me sensitive to them. When I play "Amazing Grace" I want them to feel and experience through the music the amazing grace of God, and have it make a difference in their lives.

It's truly amazing. His grace! To think that anyone can come. Though he's committed every sin in the book—if he'll only ask Jesus to come into his heart—to erase all the sin . . . *God does it.* That's His amazing grace. No wonder we sing, "How sweet the sound!"

Could John Newton have even begun to dream of how many millions he would reach with his own heart-cry of wonder and of praise? All he was doing then (in the 18th century) was uttering what Christ had done for a sinner like me. And here we are today, singing "Amazing Grace" just as heartily, just as meaningly as did the writer of this song.

So when the notes flow from my fingers I'm praying they will affect every person in that audience. When I sit down and play "He Touched Me," it's my prayer that the Holy Spirit will first touch my own heart, put me in tune with people's needs, and move me with the need of others to experience the loving touch of Jesus in their lives. People come with such burdens and cares —with such *hunger—* that nothing less than the touch of Jesus will heal and satisfy them.

I want God to touch them. I want them to *feel* His touch, to feel His very presence.

It has long been accepted that: "Music has charms to soothe

a savage beast," as the poet, William Congreve, phrased it. Apparently, Napoleon shared this view and expressed it in these words: "Music, of all the liberal arts, has the greatest influence over the passions."

In every audience there are those whose emotions are torn—by hurt, by anger, disappointments, or disillusionments. They feel forsaken; they're lonely and sad. It's my prayer that through the music as the Holy Spirit anoints and directs me, a peace, a calm, an assurance will release the turmoil in their heart.

When I play "I Walked Today Where Jesus Walked," it is my desire to *be* there. I want my audience to feel it, to walk where He walked—to experience something of His loneliness, His forsakenness—to climb the Hill of Calvary—to see Him dying there for sinners—God's great outpouring of love. If they could only know the heights of joy, to walk today where Jesus walked . . . *"And feel His presence there."*

People often come up to me at the end of a concert to express their feelings of appreciation, but can't find the words. Sometimes they may say, "It's *unreal*, Dino. It was as though words, as well as music, were coming from your fingers."

Then I know that the Spirit of God has been at work in their lives. I want it to be with my ministry as George Beverly Shea has expressed it of his, in *Then Sings My Soul:*

> Through it [the piano], I found my life's work, a way to tell others of Christ.
>
> Through it and the sacred song, I have known the mute to speak, the deaf to hear, the blind to see.

No matter who you are, let me tell you that God can use you, too. He's looking for those whom He can use. There never was a time when so many people had such great spiritual and emotional and physical needs. And they're ready to listen—they really want to *know*. As I go from place to place I find this great hunger for God. People are coming to see that nothing else has worked for them.

You don't have to look at others whom God is using, and think: *How I wish this could happen to me!*

It *can* happen to you. Believe me.

B
CLASS

5595
~~2223~~
ACC.

KARTSONAKIS
(LAST NAME OF AUTHOR)

The dino story
(BOOK TITLE)

STAMP LIBRARY OWNERSHIP

CODE 4366-03   BROADMAN SUPPLIES
CLS-3   MADE IN U.S.A.